Sociology Transformed

The field of sociology has changed rapidly over the last few decades. Sociology Transformed seeks to map these changes on a country by country basis and to contribute to the discussion of the future of the subject. The series is concerned not only with the traditional centres of the discipline, but with its many variant forms across the globe.

More information about this series at
http://www.springer.com/series/14477

Marek Skovajsa · Jan Balon

Sociology in the Czech Republic

Between East and West

palgrave
macmillan

Marek Skovajsa
Faculty of Humanities
Charles University
Prague, Czech Republic

Jan Balon
Faculty of Social Sciences
Charles University
Prague, Czech Republic

Sociology Transformed
ISBN 978-1-137-45026-5 ISBN 978-1-137-45027-2 (eBook)
DOI 10.1057/978-1-137-45027-2

Library of Congress Control Number: 2017944230

Marek Skovajsa and Jan Balon's research for this book has been supported by a Czech Science Foundation (GA ČR) grant No. 13-15802S 'From Rockefeller to Soros: the impact of American foundations on the agenda of Czech sociology' (2013–2015).

Printed on acid-free paper

This Palgrave Pivot imprint is published by Springer Nature
The registered company is Macmillan Publishers Ltd.
The registered company address is: The Campus, 4 Crinan Street, London, N1 9XW, United Kingdom

To Jiří Musil (1928–2012) and Miloslav Petrusek (1936–2012)

Acknowledgements

The authors would like to thank Christian Fleck, Uta Gerhardt, and Janusz Mucha for their extremely helpful comments. We also greatly appreciate the support and feedback from peer reviewers and series editors John Holmwood and Stephen Turner.

A special word of thanks goes to Stephan von Pohl for English-language editing of the entire manuscript. We are also grateful to the editorial team at Palgrave Macmillan, especially Philippa Grand, Tamsine O'Riordan, and Beth Farrow, for hosting this project and overseeing its completion.

Both authors gratefully acknowledge funding support from the Czech Science Foundation (GA ČR) grant No. 13-15802S 'From Rockefeller to Soros: the impact of American foundations on the agenda of Czech sociology' (2013–2015). Among other things, this funding made possible repeated visits to archives in Europe and United States as well as participation in international conferences.

Marek Skovajsa is thankful to the Rockefeller Archive Center, Sleepy Hollow, New York, for granting permission to use two citations from its materials. He is also grateful to the Masaryk Institute and Archive of the Czech Academy of Sciences, Prague, for its agreement to cite from one of its documents.

When collecting data or locating documents, we have benefited from the assistance of, in alphabetical order: Monika Baďurová, Jakub Češka, Silvia Danišová, Jiří Gruntorád, Lenka Hanovská, Radim Hladík,

Robert Klobucký, Alena Miltová, Andrea Semancová, Kateřina Spustová, Světlana Trojanová, and the librarians at the Institute of Sociology, Czech Academy of Sciences, Prague.

Finally, Marek would like to say a heartfelt thank you to Martina and Vilma for their loving support. Jan thanks Tereza and Gréta for their patience.

Contents

List of Figures

List of Tables

CHAPTER 1

Introduction: An Institutional History of Sociology in the Czech Republic

Abstract The history of sociology in the Czech Republic presented in this book is primarily focused on its institutional development. Institutionalized sociology in what today is the Czech Republic, a state created only recently (1993), has been to a large extent coterminous with Czech sociology. Whereas early Czech sociology was built around a strong sense of a political mission tied to nation- and state-building, this sense has been lost in more recent decades.

Keywords Institutional history · Nation-building · Methodological nationalism · Czech history · Sociology in the Czech Republic

The last general assembly of the 'Masaryk Czech Sociological Association' (MČSS) was held in January 2015 as a part of the biannual meeting of Czech sociologists. The conference, modest in size compared to similar meetings of other national associations (some 50 active participants divided into two parallel sessions meeting for less than 2 full days), took place at the Faculty of Social Sciences of the historic Charles University in Prague, but in an uninspiring modern building located far away from the old city center. The general assembly took its usual course until a most unexpected proposal was advanced by members of the managing board: to change the name of the association into the quite simple and profane 'Czech Sociological Association' (ČSS). Proponents argued that the association should follow the common practice of other

M. Skovajsa and J. Balon, *Sociology in the Czech Republic*, Sociology Transformed, DOI 10.1057/978-1-137-45027-2_1

national associations who are members of the International Sociological Association (ISA). Also, someone suggested that the change would put an end to confusion on the international level since many people were not sure what 'Masaryk' meant and what country the association represented. The half-sleepy atmosphere in the auditorium was suddenly transformed into a heated and lengthy debate. When the vote was eventually taken, a majority supported the name change, but the defeated minority could be heard murmuring with indignation still for some time after the conference was over....

Why are we telling this story to begin our short book about the history of sociology in the Czech Republic? We believe that it is illustrative of one of the deepest transformations that this country's sociology experienced in the course of the twentieth century. Founded as a discipline by Tomáš Garrigue Masaryk, the charismatic intellectual-cum-politician who became the first president of the Czechoslovak Republic in 1918, and further developed by his followers, Czech sociology was born with a special mission that imbued it with a sense of entitlement for widespread public respect: to guide the construction of the new nation and state. With the arrival of communist rule after WWII, both Masaryk and sociology were declared flawed and reactionary. In the 1960s, however, sociology was officially called back into existence with the expectation (again) that it would, hand in hand with economics and other social sciences, measure up to the immense task of providing directives for the reconstruction of the ailing socialist system. During the discipline's third revival after the collapse of the communist system in 1989 and the division of Czechoslovakia into the Czech Republic and Slovak Republic shortly after, the Czech government then in power—dominated as it was by an economic ideology of 'the market will solve everything'—had no interest in sociology at all. Yet as early as 1990, in an expression of their belief that a time must come when sociology would again be entrusted with the task of producing knowledge essential for society's development, Czech sociologists decided to add 'Masaryk' to their association's name. Over the course of the last 25 years, this idea of a special mission seems to have disappeared for good. But has Czech sociology really stripped itself of its innate association with nation- and state-building? To the extent that it has, has it managed to forge for itself another sense of identity and mission? These are the central questions that we will keep in mind as we move forward in telling our story.

Sociology in the Czech Republic Remains a Czech Sociology

This book is a history of sociology on the territory of what today is the Czech Republic. We have decided to refer to our subject with the turn of phrase 'sociology in the Czech Republic,' but not without acknowledging that it is a little awkward given that the time span of our narrative is much longer than the existence of this very recent state formation. We are also not quite happy with the denotation 'Czech sociology' because of the risk of an excessively narrow, methodologically nationalist interpretation of it (Beck and Sznaider 2006, pp. 3–6). However, it seems to us that, if due caution is applied, it makes—unlike in the case of some other 'sociologies in the country X'—little difference, for a number of historical reasons, to call this history a 'history of Czech sociology.'

Sociology in the Bohemian crown lands within Austria (until 1918), the Czech part of Czechoslovakia (1918–1992), and the Czech Republic (1993–present)[1] has to an overwhelming extent, and virtually without exception in the period 1945–1989 (not counting the relatively few Slovaks based at Czech institutions), been done by Czechs. This does not mean that the scope of our book is limited to sociology done by Czechs as an ethnic or national group—a decision that could rightly appear problematic to readers familiar with the complex ethnic make-up of Czechoslovakia before WWII and also in view of the existence of a *Czechoslovak* state between 1918 and 1992. But since the book's main focus is on the development of sociology as an institutionalized discipline in one particular country, it will almost exclusively discuss those organizations, individuals, groups, and intellectual products that were, in different times and places, a part of this evolving institutional reality. This approach, while, as we believe, not a priori discriminatory, places German, Slovak, and other 'non-Czech' sociologists on the outside for the simple reason that they were not involved, or were involved only marginally, in the construction of an institutionalized discipline of sociology in the Czech Republic.

Prior to WWII, the geographical area that nowadays bears the name of the Czech Republic was home to a thriving German and German-Jewish intellectual community that was a powerful competitor to but also extraordinarily stimulating for Czech academic life (see Cohen 2006). Although many German-speaking sociologists and other social scientists had some connection to this territory (e.g., Alfred Weber, Hans Zeisel, Werner Stark, or Karl W. Deutsch, to name a few), it seems to make little sense to speak in relation to it of a German-language sociology (unlike philosophy, history, legal science, literature, etc.) as an institutionalized academic discipline, or even as a relatively stable intellectual community, either in the Austrian or Czechoslovak period. There were very few German-speaking sociologists who were, for some time at least, teaching or conducting research at the country's universities or other academic institutions. Instead, they usually advanced and achieved their careers in Germany, Austria, or in the Anglo-Saxon countries.

The case of Slovak sociologists is different, but the conclusion is the same. It is certainly true that sociology in the Czech and the Slovak parts of Czechoslovakia developed in close contact for about a century, but at least since the split between the Czechs and Slovaks during WWII there have been not one, but two distinct national sociological traditions and communities (Nešpor 2011, pp. 169–188). For this reason, sociology in Slovakia remains beyond the scope of the present book. The terms 'Czechoslovakia' and 'Czechoslovak' are used when it seems historically more adequate to refer to the entire country, but we have avoided any attempts at analyzing facts pertaining to institutionalized sociology in Slovakia.

A no less important reason why Czech sociology and sociology in the Czech Republic remain largely coterminous is the limited movement of people (both in-bound and out-bound) between Czech-language sociology at Czech institutions and the outside world. To be sure, the political upheavals of the twentieth century produced several waves of emigration from Czechoslovakia (most notably in 1938, 1948, and 1968) that included sociologists as well. But the handful of sociologists of Czech origin who had an academic career in exile did not form anything like a 'Czech sociological school abroad.' The relatively insignificant outward migration of mostly young Czech sociologists after the opening of the borders since 1989 has not led to any change in this respect. All in all, the tiny Czech 'diaspora' does not show any shared set of problems and orientations or a national style of sociological work that might define a distinctly Czech tradition (see Sztompka 2010, p. 23). Conversely, as later chapters will demonstrate, participation by non-Czechs (again not counting some Slovaks) in institutionalized sociology in the Czech Republic was almost nonexistent until the 1990s and has not grown beyond the single digits ever since. Although it is no reason for celebration, we must conclude that, despite globalization, internationalization, Europeanization and the notorious critique of methodological nationalism, sociology within the borders of the Czech Republic has been and continues to be a Czech sociology, and is likely to remain such in the near future.

This does not mean that sociology in the Czech Republic is coterminous with sociology of all things Czech. It is true that the vast majority of topics on which sociologists in the Czech Republic write and do research is Czech related (Janák and Klobucký 2014). Czech sociologists probably show a lesser propensity than their American, British, or French colleagues to study social networks in Africa, interethnic conflict in Southeast Asia, or nonprofit organizations in Latin America. To some extent, this might be due to the persistence of a nation-centered mindset, but it certainly has much to do with history (among other things, Czechs were never a colonial power) and with the discipline's significantly lower resources. But, rather obviously, empirical research on non-Czech topics, broader comparative studies and generalizing theoretical thinking have been a standard part of Czech sociologists' work for decades. Reversing the perspective, one should add that, no less obviously, there has also been a long line of research on Czech subjects by sociologists from outside the Czech Republic. Especially in the roaring 1990s, sociologists from many countries of the world showed a keen interest in the topics related to the 'transformation' of Czech society (e.g., Eyal et al. 1998) and this interest has not entirely subsided. In recent years, however, it has become stronger among other social scientists, students of contemporary history, in particular.

Institutional Approach

Given the constraints on this book's length, the history of sociology in the Czech Republic which we are offering is necessarily selective. Our story looks at both the discipline's institutional and intellectual development, but it focuses more on the institutional and organizational aspects than on ideas and substance (see Turner and Turner 1990, pp. 8–9). It would be difficult, or outright impossible, to present a coherent account of the changing intellectual content of the disciplinary production in any country while completely ignoring the question of how it is embedded within the existing institutional framework. It seemed clear to us that these two objectives could not be simultaneously accomplished in such a short text, and if only one of them could, at least to some degree, then it had to be institutional history.

But since the life of any discipline is not defined by institutions alone, we also spend quite some time talking about persons, groups, publications, and even ideas (or discourse, as many readers would prefer to call the intellectual dimension). The Czech academic world is small, but not necessarily too small. It has been sufficiently large to generate an internal intellectual dynamic that has propelled a series of autonomous debates since at least the last third of the nineteenth century. Nevertheless, it is too small—and this holds *a fortiori* for Czech sociology, which has always occupied just a tiny fraction of this space—not to be dependent on intellectual input from the outside. By 'outside,' we mean first and foremost large national traditions (the most important of these have been, in approximate historical order, Austrian-German, Russian, French, British, American, and Soviet), but to these we should add today's European and global Western trends and movements. The reception and adaptation of foreign influences have thus always been an essential component of the Czech intellectual tradition, despite its sometimes excessive tendency to close itself off from the world due to national, or even nationalist, aspirations.

Applied to our subject, this means that the intellectual development of sociology in the Czech Republic can be characterized as a dual process: (1) following and selectively appropriating outside innovations and (2) generating its own momentum out of a combination of existing internal elements and foreign influences. It would nevertheless be an idealistic misconception to exaggerate the free-floating nature or autonomous dynamics of what is, after all, a complex process (see Bourdieu 1991, p. 10). Like anywhere else, the intellectual trajectory of Czech sociology has been conditioned by the institutions available to support it or regulate and constrain it (here we have another reason to take a prevailing institutional focus). Yet, in this particular case, far from enjoying any reasonable degree of autonomy, these institutions have often been heavily dependent on political power—arguably to an extent beyond what was common in most of the Western liberal democratic societies. In one important sense, the history of sociology in the Czech Republic is the history of its resilience vis-à-vis political manipulation and control.

An Outline of the Book

In the chapters that follow, the history of sociology in the Czech Republic is divided into periods primarily on the basis of the most important events in Czech political history. This choice, which is common practice among Czech authors (see Nešpor et al. 2014), has been made in conformity with the observation that, throughout its development, Czech sociology was heavily conditioned by each era's political regime. Unlike in Poland, where (as Marta Bucholc has claimed) sociology began to develop autonomously from as early as the 1950s despite external political pressures (Bucholc 2016, p. 5), Czech sociology arrived at a stage where it could be described as obeying internal, institutional, and intellectual dynamics only around the time of the communist regime's collapse in 1989. Since space limitations prevent us from providing broader contextual information about political developments in the country, we refer the reader to the most recent literature in English (Pánek and Tůma 2009; Heimann 2009).[2] A basic outline showing the milestones of Czech political history alongside the successive stages in the history of Czech sociology is presented in Table 1.1.

Even though the focus of the series 'Sociology Transformed' is on the period after 1945, we have chosen to start the history of Czech sociology from its very beginnings in the late nineteenth century. This is because its founding figures—the sociologist-presidents Tomáš G. Masaryk and Edvard Beneš, who are briefly introduced in Chap. 2 (1880s until 1918)—left a deep imprint on the discipline that did not disappear with Beneš's death in 1948. These two politicians saw sociology as a deeply 'political' science which, they claimed, provided them with guidance in their mission to build an independent Czechoslovak state. Chapter 3 offers an overview of the interwar and immediate post-WWII period (1918–1950), which witnessed significant progress in terms of sociology's institutionalization, in order to demonstrate the radical break represented by the devastating communist campaign against sociology after 1948. The early disciplinary tradition predating the dominance of Marxism-Leninism would remain a reference point (though often only implicitly so) for sociology's development during the communist and post-communist period.[3]

The four decades of communist rule (1948–1989) were characterized by numerous shifts and changes in official policy, including those

Table 1.1 Czech political history and the history of sociology

	Political history		*Sociology*
Until 1918	Czechs in Austria(-Hungary), WWI	1882–1918	T.G. Masaryk professor at the Czech University in Prague; sociologists among his students (E. Beneš)
1918	First Czechoslovak Republic	1918–1938	First institutionalization: university chairs, journals, national association
1938 1939	Munich Agreement Protectorate of Bohemia and Moravia, WWII begins	1939–1945	Closure of Czech universities; sociological journals suspended
1945	End of WWII, Czechoslovak Republic restored	1945–1950	Continuation of interwar sociology
1948	Communist takeover	1948–1956	Sociology abolished and replaced by Marxist–Leninist theory
1956	Twentieth congress of the Communist Party of the Soviet Union; Hungarian uprising, Marxist 'revisionism'	1956–1963	Sociology slowly reemerges within and out of historical materialism
1968	'Prague Spring,' invasion by Warsaw Pact countries	1964–1969	Disciplinary renewal as Marxist sociology, new departments, Institute of Sociology at the CzAS, association
1969	'Normalization' regime introduced, political purges, emigration	1969–1989	Official 'Marxist–Leninist' sociology, tough ideological control
1989	'Velvet Revolution,' collapse of communist rule	1990–	Renewal under democratic conditions; rapid expansion; new faculties, departments, journals
2004	Accession to the European Union	2000–	Internationalization and Europeanization; limited neoliberal reforms; performance-based evaluation

affecting the conditions for sociology's existence. For the sake of clarity, this period has been divided into two nearly exact halves using the climax and suppression of the Czechoslovak reform movement in 1968–1969 as the dividing point. Chapter 4 (1950–1969) describes the slow reconstitution of sociology after its eradication from academic and public life, including its memorable but short-lived comeback in the mid-1960s. The next two decades 1969–1989 (Chap. 5) are presented as a highly anomalous period marked by heavy-handed ideological control of the discipline in a country occupied by Soviet troops. The last two chapters tell the story of the discipline's renewal and transformation after 1989. In Chap. 6, we look at its reorganization against the backdrop of the profound structural, institutional, and cultural changes that swept Czech society after the demise of communism. Chapter 7 explores the challenges that sociology in the Czech Republic has faced since around 2004, when the country joined the European Union. Both chapters together put into relief the ambivalent consequences of Czech sociology's far-reaching acceptance of Western institutional and intellectual models.

It might be added that although this is a collective work, each author contributed those chapters which best correspond to his research interests. Marek Skovajsa has written Chaps. 2–5, which present the history of Czech sociology from late nineteenth century until 1989. Jan Balon bears primary responsibility for Chaps. 6 and 7, which explore the discipline's most recent fortunes from 1989 until the present. We have attempted to develop our own reading of the history of sociology in the Czech Republic, all the while engaging in a permanent conversation with earlier work on the subject but above all with an eye toward an independent scrutiny of the sources, including some previously unanalyzed archival materials and other data.

This book would have been much more difficult to write without the prior work of other sociologists and historians. Their writings are referenced throughout the book, but due to space constraints we have had to limit the number of references. We feel obliged to highlight two names from the list of our predecessors. Miloslav Petrusek (1936–2012) has done more than any other Czech sociologist to establish the study of the discipline's past as a recognized subfield after 1989. Starting in the mid-2000s, the historical literature on Czech sociology began to expand at an unusual pace thanks to the extraordinary productivity of the historian cum-sociologist and social anthropologist Zdeněk R. Nešpor (1976).[4] It is a deplorable fact, but quite symptomatic of Czech sociologists' continuing (self-)marginalization in the international circulation of ideas, that almost no text by these and other authors has been published in English or another international language.[5]

Notes

1. Some Czech historians use the methodologically nationalist term 'the Czech lands' to refer to this territory in different historical periods (Pánek and Tůma 2009).
2. These two comprehensive histories are not only the most recent ones, but they also demonstrate the disputed nature of much of their subject. Mary Heimann's controversial book has been criticized for its anti-Czech tone and a lack of factual accuracy. Despite these problems, it offers a wealth of thought-provoking interpretations and acts as an antidote to one-sidedly positive (or 'Whig,' in Heimann's terms) readings of Czech history. The volume edited by Jaroslav Pánek and Oldřich Tůma reflects the present-day mainstream view of Czech history by authors from the country's most prestigious academic institutions.
3. In applying the adjective 'communist' to the autocratic rule of the Communist Party of Czechoslovakia, we steer clear of the endless national debate in which the Left has attempted to impose the term 'state socialism' (in order to salvage 'communism' for future use) and the Right continues to defend the misnomer 'totalitarianism.'
4. Besides numerous journal articles and a book on the history of Czech sociology in the interwar period (Nešpor 2011), Nešpor recently edited and coauthored two voluminous works, a *Dictionary of Czech sociologists* and a *History of Czech sociology* (Nešpor et al. 2013, 2014), representing the most exhaustive treatment of the discipline's history in this country.
5. One notable exception is the work of Michael Voříšek, whose book on 1960s Czech sociology, *The reform generation* (Voříšek 2012), has undeservedly remained mostly unnoticed in international debates. Responsible for this neglect may be the fact that it appeared with a small Czech publishing house.

References

Beck, Ulrich, and Natan Sznaider. 2006. Unpacking cosmopolitanism for the social sciences: A research agenda. *British Journal of Sociology* 57 (1): 1–23.

Bourdieu, Pierre. 1991. The peculiar history of scientific reason. *Sociological Forum* 6 (1): 3–26.

Bucholc, Marta. 2016. *Sociology in Poland*. Basingstoke: Palgrave Macmillan.

Cohen, Gary B. 2006. *The politics of ethnic survival: Germans in Prague, 1861–1914*, 2nd ed. West Lafayette: Purdue University Press.

Eyal, Gil, Iván Szelényi, and Eleanor R. Townsley. 1998. *Making capitalism without capitalists: Class formation and elite struggles in post-communist Central Europe*. London: Verso.

Heimann, Mary. 2009. *Czechoslovakia: The state that failed*. New Haven: Yale University Press.

Janák, Dušan, and Robert Klobucký. 2014. Co bychom věděli o sociologii, kdybychom četli pouze *Sociologický časopis* a *Sociológii*? (What would we know about sociology if we only read *Sociologický časopis* and *Sociológia*?). *Sociologický časopis/Czech Sociological Review* 50 (5): 645–670.

Nešpor, Zdeněk R. 2011. *Republika sociologů. Zlatý věk české sociologie v meziválečném období a krátce po druhé světové válce* (A republic of sociologists. The golden age of Czech sociology in the interwar period and shortly after WWII). Prague: Scriptorium.

Nešpor, Zdeněk R., et al. 2013. *Slovník českých sociologů* (The dictionary of Czech sociologists). Prague: Academia.

Nešpor, Zdeněk R., et al. 2014. *Dějiny české sociologie* (The history of Czech sociology), ed. Zdeněk R. Nešpor, 121–146. Prague: Academia.

Pánek, Jaroslav, and Oldřich Tůma (eds.). 2009. *A history of the Czech lands*. Prague: Karolinum.

Sztompka, Piotr. 2010. One sociology or many? In *The ISA handbook of diverse sociological traditions*, ed. Sujata Patel, 21–28. Los Angeles: Sage.

Turner, Stephen P., and Jonathan H. Turner. 1990. *The impossible science: An institutional analysis of American sociology*. Newbury Park: Sage.

Voříšek, Michael. 2012. *The reform generation. 1960s Czechoslovak sociology from a comparative perspective*. Prague: Kalich.

CHAPTER 2

Sociology in Service to Nation-Building: The Legacy of Tomáš Garrigue Masaryk

Abstract The beginnings of Czech sociology from 1880 onward are intertwined with the academic and political career of Tomáš Garrigue Masaryk, who for 40 years was the only professor to teach the discipline at the Czech University in Prague. In Masaryk's thought, sociology was closely tied to the philosophy of history, and both were expected to provide guidelines for practical life. Masaryk and his student Edvard Beneš were early public sociologists addressing Czech society in an era of intense nationalist aspirations. Despite their claim that sociology supplied their political actions with a scientific foundation, they practiced politics as usual when they became leaders of an independent Czechoslovakia. The first institutional foundations of Czech sociology were laid before WWI, but they remained weak and fragile.

Keywords Tomáš Garrigue Masaryk · Edvard Beneš · Alice Garrigue Masaryk · Public sociology · Czech nationalism

If there were a need to justify why this chapter is centered mostly around one sole person, the answer would be that probably in no other country was the emergence of sociology the creation of a single individual to the same degree as was the case in today's Czech Republic. Tomáš Garrigue Masaryk (1850–1937) chose sociology as his academic specialty (still within philosophy) around 1880, at a time when the discipline was in its early formative stages in the large Western countries and

M. Skovajsa and J. Balon, *Sociology in the Czech Republic*, Sociology Transformed, DOI 10.1057/978-1-137-45027-2_2

an utter novelty in Austria, of which the Bohemian crown lands were one part. For the following four decades, TGM (as he is commonly called in Czech journalism and literature) supported the growth of the new discipline with great dedication. He authored the first Czech sociological writings—some of them 'expressly' sociological, many others applying 'a sociological way of thinking' (Nový 1968, p. 300)—used his scholarly and political weight to elevate the standing of this subject, and lectured on sociological themes to several generations of enthusiastic students. If the influence of Masaryk the political leader on Czech society cannot be overestimated, the same applies to the influence of Masaryk the sociologist on Czech sociology. The first Czech sociological association, founded in 1925, would be called the Masaryk Sociological Society still in his lifetime.

Any account of the origins of Czech sociology cannot ignore its wide-ranging extra-academic portfolio, which makes this discipline look similar in some respects, and very different in other respects, to sociological traditions in the core Western countries. As in these other countries, there was a close connection between sociology and social reformism of a socialist or religious nature, or even both at the same time (see, e.g., Turner 2014, Chap. 1). Yet, very much unlike in the large countries of the West, Czech sociology was intimately wedded, through the person of Masaryk and his followers, to the project of the cultural, social, and political emancipation of the Czech nation. This expectation that sociology should play a political role and make a concrete contribution to the nationalist cause was present from the very beginning of the discipline's history in Czech society. It further grew in intensity when nation-building seamlessly turned into state-building after the defeat of Austria-Hungary in WWI in 1918, which provided a unique historical opportunity for Czechoslovak independence.

Masaryk's Sociological Work

Even a devoted admirer of Masaryk such as the American sociologist Earle Edward Eubank had to admit as early as 1 year after Masaryk's death that his 'importance as a sociologist is almost forgotten by the sociologists themselves' (Eubank 1938, p. 456), a statement that was virtually repeated by Alan Wolfe half a century later (Wolfe in Masaryk 1994, p. ix). The main reasons which Eubank cited for this early forgetting of Masaryk the sociologist as opposed to Masaryk the political man were TGM's service as 'the founder of a State,' 'liberator of a people,' and the four-times elected President of Czechoslovakia (this multiple election was but one of the worrisome features of a political system that was the only democracy in Central Europe in the 1930s, not in the smallest measure due to Masaryk's influence, but that still had its fair share of shortcomings, see Bugge 2007). The argument that Masaryk was too successful in political affairs to be remembered mainly for his academic contributions might be plausible, but it leaves unanswered the question of Masaryk's real stature as a sociologist.

In relation to Masaryk's contribution to academic sociology, three points seem to be especially important: (1) Even though Masaryk is the author of a vast and brilliant body of work, all of which bears some sociological relevance, he left a rather limited legacy in the domain of what sociology was to become later in his lifetime and after his death; (2) Some of Masaryk's principal philosophical and sociological ideas (he distinguished between these two but saw them as intimately interrelated) are deeply ambivalent or outright contradictory, a fact that might have endowed these ideas with their extraordinary vitality in practical political life but that at the same time represented obstacles to the development of Czech sociology after Masaryk; (3) While Masaryk's role as both the intellectual and institutional founder of Czech sociology is beyond dispute, his forceful, multifaceted personality (radiating what Roman Szporluk aptly called the 'Masaryk mystique'—1981, p. 237, fn. 59), and political clout were more important factors in helping the newly established discipline achieve a certain status than his intellectual contribution to sociology per se (for a related discussion regarding Masaryk as a philosopher, see Kohák 2008, Chap. 4).

As a matter of fact, because of the eminently practical bent of his personality, Masaryk produced only a handful of texts that can be classified as pure academic sociology. Far from being a disengaged objective study, his early monograph on suicide[1] (*Suicide as mass social phenomenon of modern civilization*, first edition in German 1881), which was accepted as his *Habilitationsschrift* in philosophy at the University of Vienna, amounts to a passionate indictment of the moral and religious malaise of the modern age for which, as is characteristic of Masaryk, he sought to find a remedy in a new form of enlightened religion derived from Protestantism (see Giddens 1970). Almost immediately after his move to Prague in 1882 to assume the chair of philosophy ('I would actually have preferred a chair in sociology, but Austria had no such chair at the time,' Masaryk and Čapek 1995, p. 91) at the newly established Czech branch of the University of Prague, Masaryk became deeply embroiled in the political struggles of the emerging Czech nation, which continued to occupy him for the rest of his long life.

This came at no small price for Masaryk the academic sociologist: his most ambitious epistemological treatise, *The fundamentals of concrete logic* (1885, revised German edition 1887), in which he gave expression to the psychologism underlying his conception of sociology, was written hastily during a holiday (Masaryk and Čapek 1995, p. 111). His second and final attempt at working out the epistemological and methodological foundations of the discipline, the *Handbook of sociology* (1900), which appeared as a series of journal articles, remained unfinished. For Masaryk's substantive sociological contributions, one has to peruse his many works in religious philosophy, cultural history and political theory, as well as his political pamphlets. To be sure, Masaryk considered any of these writings sociological as long as they involved the element of unprejudiced 'scientific' analysis of social and historical facts (an approach he and his followers called 'critical realism'). In that sense, most of his work is sociological. But from the vantage point of how academic sociology was to evolve later, it is fair to conclude that sociological writing makes up only a small fraction of the prolific output of the founder of Czech sociology (Nový 1968).

Masaryk and Beneš: Public Sociologists, or Politicians?

Like many other sociologists of his era, Masaryk was a social reformer. One might even say that he fits the mold of the Anglo-American reform-oriented social scientists, influenced as he was by his New England wife Charlotte Garrigue and his numerous connections overseas. But he was, above all, a Central European political leader, or to put it more dramatically, a fighter for national independence who became the founder of a new country, something that very few other sociologists came close to in his or any other time. In no small measure, Masaryk's writings are imbued with a philosophy of history that provides intellectual justification for his nationalist political program. As one of Masaryk's much younger contemporaries Karel Galla aptly commented (1968, p. 278), for Masaryk sociology was 'a link mediating between philosophy and practice.' As can be seen in his *Fundamentals of concrete logic*, he considered the philosophy of history to be a part of sociology already in the early stages of his intellectual development:

> Questions as to teleology and the rationale of development are relegated by some sociologists to the realm of metaphysics. ... I can now briefly state that it is sociology that should examine all these questions rather than some supra-scientific 'philosophy' or 'metaphysics' of history. Of course I have nothing against terminology; what is always involved is a proper understanding of the meaning of philosophy of history as a part of sociology and not as a science or a portion of philosophy apart from and above sociology. (Masaryk 1994, p. 112)

In his writings on the Czech nation, Masaryk developed a religiously based philosophy of history which relied on the assumption that the fates of national collectivities are ruled by Providence, which sides with those nations that are committed to the ideal of democratic humanism (Masaryk 1994, pp. 280, 292). Here the most problematic side of Masaryk's legacy comes to light: in his oeuvre sociology, philosophical speculation, historical construction, religious conviction, political campaign, and moral crusade mix inextricably; statement of fact is followed by judgment of value, and all of this is confusingly clad in a language that is, to a large extent, borrowed from positivist scientism. This was the criticism made against Masaryk by some of his opponents in the long debate on the 'meaning of Czech history,' launched in 1895 by the publication of Masaryk's historical-political study *The Czech question* and involving some of the most prominent Czech intellectuals of several consecutive generations—though, incidentally, very few sociologists (Havelka 1995, 1999, p. 234).

Masaryk and his closest disciple in both sociology and politics, Edvard Beneš, can be seen as exemplars of early 'public sociologists,' but this anachronistic label should not be taken too far. Using Michael Burawoy's influential distinction, it is possible to argue that, under Austrian domination, Masaryk and Beneš represented both the traditional and the organic type of public sociologists. They were members of the educated national elite who, with their academic writings, journalism and political activities, aimed to shape the public debate as traditional public sociologists do. But viewed from another angle, they were intellectuals organically connected to the Czechs who were one of the 'subject people,' to cite Eubank again (1938, p. 460), of the Austro-Hungarian empire.

If the organic public sociologist as described by Burawoy (2005, p. 7) 'works in close connection with a visible, thick, active, local and often counterpublic,' then this is exactly what Masaryk and Beneš were doing in the years before WWI, when the 'organic' or 'small-scale work' and the 'socialization' of Czech nation formed the centerpiece of TGM's political program (Masaryk 1994, pp. 290, 334; Havelka 1999, p. 228, fn. 3). But when a spectacular twist of fate catapulted Masaryk and Beneš in 1918 into the position of the two most powerful political leaders of their newly established country, it no longer seems appropriate to place them in the category of public sociologists. They have suddenly been made rulers, and this transformation could not fail to create a deep conflict with their sociological identity.

Masaryk served as President of Czechoslovakia from 1918 until 1935. Beneš was Minister of Foreign Affairs or Prime Minister during Masaryk's tenure and President from 1935 until 1948, with a wartime interruption which he mostly spent as the head of the Czechoslovak exile government in London. During all this time, they never ceased to maintain that their political actions rested on a scientific fundament provided by sociology. Beneš characterized the shared foundations of their political practice using words that unambiguously reveal his belief that good politics were based on 'sociological training, the self-conscious practicing of politics as practical sociology, the consistent application of the scientific method of sociology, supplemented, to be sure, by a philosophy and a philosophy of history…' (Beneš 1936, p. 16). Yet, this quote also shows that, like Masaryk, Beneš thought that practical action needs to be governed by a bold historical vision which could not be supplied by scientific sociology alone. It takes, he stressed, a philosophy of history for a politician to achieve greatness (ibid., p. 10).

In actual practice, however, both Masaryk and Beneš were prone to making concessions to *Realpolitik* that were bigger than they would be willing to acknowledge. In his struggle for Czechoslovak independence during WWI and then as president, Masaryk often strategized and used propaganda in order to maximize his chances for success; he did not shy away from petty politicking and consciously fostered the cult of his own person (Klimek 2002; Orzoff 2009). As a political leader, he had to make decisions that could not equally satisfy every group of Czechoslovak citizens, and some of these groups felt aggravated more deeply than others: Germans, Slovaks, Catholics, communists. His successor Beneš was to face even greater political dilemmas as

Czechoslovakia's president. Notoriously controversial are his decisions not to defend the country against Hitler in September 1938, to expel the Sudeten Germans in 1945, and to hand political power over to the Communist Party in 1948. It would be difficult to show—and would certainly not reflect favorably on sociology—that these hard choices (inasmuch as they were choices at all) were based on a 'scientific' sociological fundament.

Despite these reservations, it would not be fair to Masaryk and Beneš to see them as cut-and-dried politicians and to write off the country which they created as nothing more than 'the state that failed' (Heimann 2009). Interwar Czechoslovakia had an imperfect, nationally biased, democracy ('nationalism with a human face' as Szporluk (1981) called it), but it was still a democracy whose liberal climate attracted emigration from Red Russia (including Pitirim Sorokin, Georges Gurvitch, and Roman Jakobson) in the 1920s and from Germany and Austria in the 1930s. Until it lost its own independence, Czechoslovakia served as a temporary haven and escape route for German and Austrian Jews and antifascists (Becher and Heumos 1992). The cult of TGM was excessive and, in its extreme forms, even tasteless. But Masaryk also commanded genuine respect from many leading minds of the time, sociologists included. 'It is astonishing,' remarked Leopold von Wiese when Masaryk turned 80, 'how much has been written on the thought and action of this great scholar and statesman' (von Wiese in Mertl 1931/1932, p. 110).

Laying the Institutional Foundations

Czech sociology before independence in 1918 existed mostly in and through the person of Masaryk and his circle of collaborators, students, and followers (see Nešpor 2014). The only university at which 7 million Czech speakers could study humanities and social sciences in the Czech language (the latter, sociology included, only in an inchoate form) was the Czech branch of the ancient University of Prague. Neither the university's Czech, nor its German branch had a chair of sociology. Sociology was taught only because Masaryk, who held a chair in philosophy, dedicated some of his lectures to sociological topics. He gave his first course on 'Practical philosophy built on a foundation of sociology' in the 1884/1885 academic year—3 years before Emile Durkheim held his first lectures on sociology in France. But there was no study program or degree in sociology until well after 1918. In the years preceding WWI, this absence was partially remedied through self-help activities, most importantly in the joint sociological section, founded in 1911, of the Union of Czechoslovak Students and the Association of Academically Educated Women, which was led by TGM's daughter, Alice Masaryk, herself an 'applied sociologist.' Alice Masaryk, who was half-American from her mother's side, spent over a year in 1904/1905 at the University of Chicago Social Settlement, where she became acquainted with, among others, Jane Addams, Charles Richmond Henderson, and George Herbert Mead. Deeply influenced by the spirit of Chicago social reformism, she became a leading figure in the development of social work and public health in the Bohemian lands and later in Czechoslovakia. Yet, despite possessing training that was equal or superior to that of her male colleagues, she could not aspire to any career in the still exclusively masculine world of Czech academic sociology (Lovčí 2008, pp. 63–67, 111–116; Keith 1991).

The discipline's position at the Czech University in Prague improved shortly before WWI, when two of Masaryk's students received their *venia legendi*, both in philosophy but with a focus on sociology. The first of these, Břetislav Foustka (1862–1947) was made a *docent* [2] in 1905 and went on to become an important figure in the subsequent institutional expansion of Czech sociology. Foustka was a leading member of abstinence and anti-prostitution associations as well as of clubs for the Czech intellectual elite. His most important contribution to the field was the book, *The weak in human society* (Foustka 1904), which offered a criticism of Social Darwinism from the standpoint of Masaryk's humanistic philosophy, and a translation of Franklin Giddings' treatise *The principles of sociology* (1900), which for almost three decades was the only translation of any important work of American sociology available in the Czech language.

The second of Masaryk's protégés to receive a habilitation at the Czech University in Prague was Edvard Beneš (1884–1948). Beneš was productive as an academic writer in his early years, culminating in a book on political parties that formed the basis for his promotion to docent in 1913 (Beneš 1912; Olivová 1998). Treading closely in TGM's footsteps, after the outbreak of WWI he went into exile to France where he soon became one of the leaders of the Czechoslovak independence movement. Diplomacy and politics were to remain his principal roles for the rest of his life.

All in all, Czech sociology before 1918 was a growing discipline whose assets included Masaryk, two *private docents*, several younger academics (the most prominent of whom will be introduced in the next chapter), and a relatively large pool of followers among university students. This notwithstanding, the discipline was still far from full academic institutionalization, as documented by the complaints presented in the middle of WWI by Emanuel Chalupný, one of sociology's most fervent promoters:

> The holdings of sociological literature in the largest Austrian libraries are quite haphazard and incomplete: the Prague library is short of more than a half, the library of Vienna of at least a third of the principal writings from this discipline, not to speak about the less important writings. There are no specialized libraries for sociology (such as those belonging to a university seminar). And it is needless especially in this difficult time to describe what kind of difficulties confront those wishing to supply themselves with academic literature from abroad. In this situation, when the school directives do not care about systematic training in sociology, when even those individuals showing an especially zealous dedication to this science lack the aids needed to follow its steps in an appropriate manner, and when even docents of sociology are forced to apply for habilitation under the broad label of philosophy or similar, one should not be surprised that in sociology the doors are wide open to empty clichés and charlatanism.... (Chalupný 1916, quoted in Voráček 1999, p. 113)

Unlike other Central European countries, where some of the most important representatives of early sociology were Marxists (e.g., Kazimierz Kelles-Krauz and Ludwik Krzywicki in Poland or Otto Bauer and Karl Renner in Austria), in the Czech case sociology and Marxism were almost completely separate from each other. When the communist-era historian of sociology Antonín Vaněk attempted to construct a history of Czech Marxist sociology, he had to content himself with a handful of rather marginal figures from the interwar period (Vaněk 1985, pp. 72–76). This distance between sociology and Marxism resulted from the political orientation of Masaryk himself, who, to be sure, tended toward socialism, but his was a socialism of an outspokenly reformist and religious-based kind. Masaryk opposed historical materialism, the idea of a revolutionary overhaul of the social order, and the Marxist critique of religion in many of his writings, most systematically in *The social question* (1898), his influential two-volume dissection of the 'crisis of Marxism.'

Since sociology was, so to speak, 'Masaryk's science,' very few adherents of this new discipline showed Marxist inclinations; and, conversely, the supporters of Marxism had little respect either for Masaryk or for sociology.

Conclusion

Though it was in great part rhetorical, the alliance between positivist scientism and the philosophy of history on which Masaryk's sociology was built is one of the most productive but also potentially deleterious aspects of his work. The productivity of this alliance was pointed out by Lubomír Nový (1968, p. 305), according to whom the 'dual character' of Masaryk's sociology paved the way for two distinct types of sociological development: the rise of empirical social research and the cultivation of an interest in sociology among Czech philosophers, theologians and, one may add, historians. This is no doubt true, but it is also the case that the view of sociology as just a more sophisticated form of the philosophy of history (which differs from unscientific philosophies of history in that it is pursued by an educated critical mind) and the prestige lent to this conception by the figure of TGM has hindered the development of Czech sociology ever since international sociology moved beyond its speculative-philosophical stage. The extremely broad and diluted view of sociology that became encoded in the Masarykian tradition persisted among his followers well after TGM's death and led to a sharp conflict with younger proponents of sociology as an empirical science. In the eyes of the public, sociology was roughly equivalent to the academically informed pursuit of political goals in the service of Czech nation—and state-building.

It would not, of course, be fair to place all the blame for this state of affairs on Masaryk alone. His fate was that of a dominant founding father whose intellectual descendants were unable to emancipate themselves from him in due time as a condition of the discipline's further progress. The specific problem of Czech sociology in the first half of the twentieth century was that Masaryk's extraordinary status as a politician and national symbol made it virtually impossible for his sociological progeny to step out of his long shadow. Masaryk's authority was one of the main factors that maintained the generation of his students in positions of power and influence for a very long time, keeping his students' students in a subordinate position. Hence, unlike for instance the United

States during the interwar years, where younger sociologists successfully challenged the older generation (Turner 2007, p. 139), Czech sociology in the same period saw much generational conflict but little personnel replacement across generational lines. This is one of the stories that will be told in the next chapter.

Notes

1. In the Czech literature, this book is generally considered to mark the birth of Czech sociology. It should be noted that the most important figure of the proto-sociological period preceding Masaryk was the Czech-German educationalist Gustav Adolf Lindner (1828–1887). Almost forgotten today, Lindner was the author of widely used textbooks for Austrian high schools, which made him influential over whole generations of students, including Sigmund Freud and Georg Simmel. His handbook of psychology was a popular textbook at late nineteenth-century US colleges (Jahoda 2007, pp. 57–62; Roucek 1945, p. 718).
2. In accordance with a Central European tradition inspired by the German academic model, at Czech universities a *docent* has been an academic title that enables its holder to give university lectures in a particular discipline. From the late nineteenth century onward, the title was awarded by the professors of a faculty (subject to approval by the ministry of education) in a procedure known as *habilitation*, which entailed the submission of a scholarly publication and a formal lecture. Most docents were unsalaried *private docents*, not entitled, unlike full professors who were state servants, to any remuneration except for student fees for their lectures (Durdík 1893, p. 745).

References

Becher, Peter, and Peter Heumos (eds.). 1992. *Drehscheibe Prag. Zur deutschen Emigration in der Tschechoslowakei 1933–1939.* München: Oldenbourg.

Beneš, Edvard. 1912. *Strannictví: sociologická studie* (Political partisanship: A sociological study). Prague: Forejtek and Beneš.

Beneš, Edvard. 1936. Sociolog-teoretik a politik-praktik (Theoretical sociologist and practical politician). *Sociologická revue* 7 (1–2): 7–20.

Bugge, Peter. 2007. Czech democracy 1918–1938—Paragon or parody? *Bohemia* 47 (1): 3–28.

Burawoy, Michael. 2005. For public sociology. *American Sociological Review* 70 (1): 4–28.

Chalupný, Emanuel. 1916. O nynějším stavu sociologie (On current state of sociology). *Národní listy* 2 April (92): 11.

Durdík, Petr [PD]. 1893. Docent. In *Ottův slovník naučný* (Otto's encyclopaedia), vol. VII, 745. Prague: J. Otto.

Eubank, Earle Edward. 1938. Thomas Garrigue Masaryk: Sociologist. *Social Forces* 16 (4): 455–462.

Foustka, Břetislav. 1904. *Slabí v lidské společnosti: ideály humanitní a degenerace národů* (The weak in human society: Humanistic ideals and the degeneration of nations). Prague: Jan Laichter.

Galla, Karel. 1968. Vývojové tendence české sociologie (Developmental tendencies of Czech sociology). *Sociologický časopis* 4 (3): 273–287.

Giddens, Anthony. 1970. Introduction. In Thomas G. Masaryk, *Suicide and the meaning of civilization*, xix–xli. Chicago: University of Chicago Press.

Havelka, Miloš (ed.). 1995. *Spor o smysl českých dějin 1895–1938* (The controversy about the meaning of Czech history). Prague: Torst.

Havelka, Miloš. 1999. Tschechische Soziologie im gesellschaftlichen Wandel. *Jahrbuch für Soziologiegeschichte 1995*, 223–253. Opladen: Leske + Budrich.

Heimann, Mary. 2009. *Czechoslovakia: The state that failed*. New Haven: Yale University Press.

Jahoda, Gustav. 2007. *A history of social psychology: From the eighteenth-century enlightenment to the Second World War*. Cambridge: Cambridge University Press.

Keith, Bruce. 1991. Alice Masaryk (1879–1966). In *Women in sociology*, ed. Mary Jo Deegan, 298–305. Westport, CT: Greenwood Press.

Klimek, Antonín. 2002. *Velké dějiny zemí Koruny české XIV, 1929–1938* (Great history of the Lands of the Bohemian Crown XIV, 1929–1938). Prague, Litomyšl: Paseka.

Kohák, Erazim. 2008. *Hearth and horizon: Cultural identity and global humanity in Czech philosophy*. Prague: Filosofia.

Lovčí, Radovan. 2008. *Alice Garrigue Masaryková: život ve stínu slavného otce* (Alice Garrigue Masaryk: A life in the shadow of the famous father). Prague: Togga.

Masaryk, Thomas Garrigue. 1994. *Constructive sociological theory: Forgotten legacy of Thomas G. Masaryk*, ed. Alan Woolfolk and Jonathan B. Imber. New Brunswick, NJ: Transaction Publishers.

Masaryk, Thomas Garrigue, and Karel Čapek. 1995. *Talks with T.G. Masaryk*, ed. Michael Henry Heim, trans. Dora Round. North Haven, CT: Cat Bird Press.

Mertl, Jan. 1931/1932. Neuerscheinungen aus der tschechischen soziologischen Literatur. *Kölner Vierteljahrshefte für Soziologie* 10: 110–117.

Nešpor, Zdeněk R. 2014. Česká sociologie před první světovou válkou (Czech sociology before WWI). In *Dějiny české sociologie* (The history of Czech sociology), ed. Zdeněk R. Nešpor, 39–63. Prague: Academia.

Nový, Lubomír. 1968. Masaryk jako sociolog (Masaryk as a sociologist). *Sociologický časopis* 4 (3): 297–306.

Olivová, Věra. 1998. Univerzitní dráha Edvarda Beneše (Edvard Beneš's university career). In Edvard Beneš, *Přednášky na Univerzitě Karlově 1913–1948* (Lectures at Charles University, 1913–1948), 9–32. Prague: Společnost Edvarda Beneše.

Orzoff, Andrea. 2009. *Battle for the castle: The myth of Czechoslovakia in Europe, 1914–1948*. Oxford: Oxford University Press.

Roucek, Joseph S. 1945. Czechoslovak sociology. In *Twentieth century sociology*, ed. Georges Gurvitch and Wilbert Ellis Moore, 717–731. New York: Philosophical Library.

Szporluk, Roman. 1981. Masaryk's republic: Nationalism with a human face. In *T.G. Masaryk in perspective: Comments and criticism*, ed. Milič Čapek and Karel Hrubý, 219–239. Ann Arbor, MI: SVU Press.

Turner, Stephen. 2007. A life in the first half-century of sociology: Charles Ellwood and the division of sociology. In *Sociology in America: A history*, ed. Craig Calhoun, 115–154. Chicago: University of Chicago Press.

Turner, Stephen. 2014. *American sociology: From pre-disciplinary to post-normal*. Basingstoke: Palgrave Macmillan.

Vaněk, Antonín. 1985. *Kapitoly z dějin české a slovenské sociologie* (Chapters from the history of Czech and Slovak sociology). Prague: Charles University.

Voráček, Emil. 1999. Emanuel Chalupný, problémy rozvoje sociologie v Československu 20. let a vznik Masarykovy sociologické společnosti (Chalupný, the problems related to the development of sociology in 1920s Czechoslovakia and the establishment of Masaryk Sociological Society). In *Emanuel Chalupný, česká kultura, česká sociologie a Tábor*, ed. Josef Zumr, 107–130. Prague: Filosofia.

CHAPTER 3

A False Beginning? The Growth and Destruction of Czech Sociology 1918–1950

Abstract The institutionalization of sociology made big steps forward in the newly independent Czechoslovak state after 1918. The first professors were appointed, sociology became a recognized academic discipline, and a national association was founded. Two antagonistic centers crystalized at the universities in Prague and Brno, each of which launched its own sociological journal. The most consequential tension in the interwar years, however, was that between the philosophical sociology of the adherents of Masaryk and the empirical sociology promoted by the younger cohort born around 1900. Sociology experienced another expansion after Liberation in 1945. Yet, despite having socialist inclinations, the discipline was crushed by the communist powerholders after 1948.

Keywords Inocenc Arnošt Bláha · Otakar Machotka · Zdeněk Ullrich Masaryk Sociological Society · First Czechoslovak Republic (1918–1938) People's democracies

Students of the history of Czech sociology are familiar with the enthusiastic words which Howard Becker used to assess the state of the discipline in Czechoslovakia shortly before the outbreak of WWII: '… there is no country anywhere of equal size that can display so impressive a list of contemporary sociologists or such a range and intensity of sociological activity' (Becker and Barnes [1938] 1961, p. 1067).

M. Skovajsa and J. Balon, *Sociology in the Czech Republic*, Sociology Transformed, DOI 10.1057/978-1-137-45027-2_3

In retrospect, it is obvious that Becker's assessment became obsolete soon after it left the printers: sociology was heavily hit by the closure of Czech universities that was a part of the assault on the country's intellectual elite during the Nazi occupation in 1939–1945; worse still, the communists' rise to power after 1945 resulted in sociology being completely abolished and banished from official academic life. But Becker's words are somewhat inflated even if taken to refer only to the period before 1938. In this chapter, we show that sociology attained a relatively advanced stage of institutionalization in interwar Czechoslovakia, but we also argue that the potential for its expansion and growth was severely constrained. The factors behind this were not only the proverbial inertia of Central European academic institutions or the shortage of resources that the newly founded state was able and willing to spend on the development of a new discipline; the principal source of this limitation was internal: the persistence of the Masarykian conception of sociology, which remained wedded to the project of Czech nation- and state-building.

The literature on sociology in the First Czechoslovak Republic (1918–1938) has often emphasized the antagonism between two geographical centers: the universities in Prague and Brno (Nešpor 2011; Janák 2013). It might seem that this polarity can, in large measure, be accounted for by the rivalry between the capital, Prague, and the regional center, Brno, or, more appropriately, by the complex dynamics of center-periphery relations within a nation-state. But, in fact, this geographical tension is of secondary importance. The conflict which defined the character and delimited the possibilities of interwar Czech sociology was the one between those who saw sociology as applied social philosophy in service of the national community, often with a moralizing and religious-based agenda, and those who wanted to practice sociology as an 'objective,' secular, and empirical social science (see Petrusek 2002, p. 10). This was to a large extent a generational issue, pitting the students and followers of Tomáš G. Masaryk, born around 1890 or earlier, against the younger cohort born around 1900, which drew inspiration from the discipline's development in the most advanced Western countries.

Two preliminary remarks are in place. First, concepts such as 'Czech' sociology or 'Czech' universities are anachronistic in reference to the interwar period, for in accordance with the official ideology of the Czechoslovak state which Czech sociologists adhered to without exception, universities, academic disciplines, journals, and so on were Czechoslovak. But since we focus on sociological activities and institutions located within what much later will become the Czech Republic and the role played by the Slovaks in this domain was limited, it is more appropriate to speak of 'Czech' sociology. This framework also precludes any systematic study of sociology pursued by Czechoslovak Germans and other national groups, who were mostly active outside Czechoslovakia. Second, women continued to be excluded from advanced university degrees, academic jobs, and the leadership of the sociological community. Nevertheless, some signs of a coming change became visible overtime. The number of female students was on the increase, trained female sociologists took part in various empirical research projects, and even the male-dominated sociological journals began to show some openness toward women (see Nešpor 2011, pp. 242–244).

The Expansion of Sociology at Czech Universities After 1918

For Czech sociology, the interwar years were a period of major advancement in terms of institutional development and stabilization. This was the case especially in the domain of higher education.[1] The new Masaryk University in Brno became home to a second center of Czech sociology that soon matched and, in some respects, overshadowed Prague in importance when a sociological seminar (the approximate equivalent of what today is a department) was opened there in 1922 under the direction of the most hardworking and dedicated Czech sociologist of the interwar period, Inocenc Arnošt Bláha (1879–1960), appointed professor in 1924. Bláha, who had established his sociological credentials before WWI, was the proponent of a somewhat updated version of Masaryk's 'critical realism.' What differentiated him most clearly from Masaryk was his interest in empirical social research, which Bláha conducted by himself or jointly with his students. Bláha also had a knack for social theorizing, as documented by the more abstract sections of his books and articles and by his posthumously published compendium, *Sociology* (Bláha 1968). He elaborated his own version of functionalist social theory, summarized under the title of 'federative functionalism' (federative as opposed to hierarchical), which was based on the idea that every social function is the fulfillment of a specific need arising in a concrete social situation (Obrdlíková 1970; Janák 2009, pp. 123–148).

Still, there were also clear limits to his empirical and theoretical work. A moralist and popular educator by inclination, though also as a result of the unpropitious social and cultural conditions prevailing in Czech society in his early lifetime, he shared with Masaryk a strongly ethical and engaged conception of sociology that resulted in much of his work having an exhortative and didactic character.

Despite these limitations, Bláha's seminal contribution to Czech sociology is beyond doubt. A prolific writer as well as a dedicated teacher and organizer of academic life, Bláha soon converted his seminar into a thriving center of training and research that attracted talented young people seriously interested in sociology. The long duration and systematic style of Bláha's academic efforts—he held the chair of sociology for almost 30 years, interrupted only by the Nazi occupation—helped to create the phenomenon known as the 'Brno sociological school'—several generations of Bláha's students who adopted their mentor's approach to addressing theoretical and empirical questions of social life.

Bláha's exceptional commitment to his discipline and his seminar in Brno can be illustrated with the story of American sociologist Earle E. Eubank's study visit to Czechoslovakia (Käsler 1991, pp. 95–99). After a vain attempt to meet any representative of Czech sociology in Prague, Eubank was enthusiastically welcomed at the train station in Brno by Bláha holding a recent issue of the *American Journal of Sociology*. Their first meeting resulted in a friendship and in an excessively enthusiastic picture of Czechoslovak sociology, as painted by Eubank in his reports for the American professional audience (e.g., Eubank 1936, p. 151). Through his contacts to Eubank and a long list of other foreign sociologists, Bláha greatly contributed to placing Czech sociology on the international map.

It is in connection with Brno's Masaryk University that Emanuel Chalupný (1879–1958), another prominent representative of Czech sociology in the interwar period, should be mentioned. A cantankerous and eccentric figure, Chalupný obtained his habilitation in sociology in Brno with Bláha's assistance after similar attempts in Prague and Bratislava had failed. Chalupný wrote the first Czech *Introduction to sociology* (Chalupný 1905), but above all he is the author of an ambitious 'system of sociology' envisioned as consisting of 12 volumes, of which 10 volumes were published. In addition, he penned several dozen shorter books and booklets on a broad range of topics, most of them with some sociological relevance. The sheer quantity of his published output earned him the nickname 'Chalupný the Voluminous' (Becker in Becker and Barnes [1938] 1961, p. 1064), but the academic reception of his ideas, which reflected the state of the discipline from the time when Masaryk left for politics (meaning around 1900), was mixed at best. Chalupný's work was seen critically by the younger generation of Czech sociologists for the same reasons that Luther L. and Jessie S. Bernard expressed in their review of his *Précis d'un système de sociologie* (Chalupný 1930): 'It is mainly logical, somewhat apologetic, and for the most part old-fashioned. Chalupný is concerned with definition, history, relations among the social sciences, laws, statics and dynamics, environment and product, but always in the abstract' (1933, p. 288).

The prospects for sociology were simultaneously more promising and more difficult in Prague. Stronger competition among individuals and proximity to political power resulted in worse rather than better conditions for academic activity. The first professor of sociology at Prague's Charles University was appointed in 1919 (Břetislav Foustka), and a sociological seminar under his direction opened in the same year.[2] Foustka, who was almost 60 at the time, probably did his best to carry the burdens of this and his many other offices, but he could not match Bláha's energetic enthusiasm. In 1923, a second professor of sociology was appointed at Charles University—Minister of Foreign Affairs, Edvard Beneš, but except for several short stints he was too busy in politics to find any time to teach. As a result, for most of the 1920s Prague had two professors of sociology, but neither of them showed the degree of dedication needed to give the new discipline a boost. This situation changed somewhat for the better in 1932, when Josef Král (1882–1978) replaced Foustka as professor and soon also as the head of the sociological seminar (Nešpor 2014, pp. 123–124; Voráček 1999, p. 115). Like Foustka and Beneš, Král was a follower of Masaryk, although he kept a greater distance from his mentor than his colleagues. He was not a sociologist, unless the term is taken in the broadest Masarykian sense; his specialty was the history of Czech philosophy and of the sociologizing currents within it. Král's contribution to the development of Czech sociology consisted mainly in his support for the ambition of the younger cohort of academics to practice the discipline as a truly empirical science (see Nešpor 2011, p. 138).

For a period when no study programs in today's sense existed, the extent to which a discipline had become institutionalized within the university system can be estimated by the number and particular characteristics of university professorships (chairs), habilitations and doctorates, as well as by the number of students taking courses or examinations and writing dissertations in the chosen discipline. By 1938, there were five ordinary and extraordinary professors of sociology at Czech universities and a dozen private docents. Reliable data concerning the number of students enrolled in sociology courses in the interwar period are not available, but anecdotal evidence shows that sociology was a popular subject.[3] Sociology was granted the right to hold the so-called 'rigorous examinations' (a prerequisite for being awarded the title of *philosophiae doctor*, PhDr., which is unique to Central Europe and as such should not be mistaken for the Anglo-American Ph.D.) in Prague in 1931 and in Brno in 1936. By 1940, around 40 students have taken a rigorous examination in sociology and over 50 students have submitted a dissertation on a sociological topic either in Prague or in Brno (Nešpor 2012, pp. 671–682). Sociology found firm footing at the universities, but its academic prestige was lower than that of more traditional disciplines.

The Emergence of Other Disciplinary Institutions

Although much of the Czechoslovak system of higher education after 1918 was brand new, in many aspects the organizational structure and culture at Czechoslovak universities were a continuation of the old Austrian ways (see Petráň 1983, pp. 321–324). The Faculties of Philosophy (or 'Arts') where sociology found its home were considered—and not just by insiders—the sacred domain of humanities scholars. Sociology, with its practical interests and need for costly research funding, was an odd fellow in this traditionalist environment. Despite containing some gross simplifications, the following passage from Otakar Machotka's essay on *American Sociology* provides what can be seen as a realistic portrayal of the typical Czech mandarin (here subsumed under the broader concept of a 'European scholar' and contrasted to his US counterpart):

> The surprising development of American sociology is due to special conditions, which differ from the European conditions of scientific work. The first of the different conditions is the *personality* of the American scholar. From the physical point of view he does not differ from other Americans; he is not as nervous, absent-minded, unaccustomed to physical work and

> removed from practical life as the European scholar. His work ... is regular, well organized, using much money, physical means and collaborators, following a detailed plan. The European scholar follows more internal stimuli, works irregularly, frequently modifies his ideas and written texts. He awaits inspiration and his work is conceived more or less as a creation. (Machotka 1938, p. 75; original English revised; emphasis original)

With the possibilities of sociology's growth at the universities clearly circumscribed by financial constraints, resistance from the conservative academic milieu and the jealousies of other disciplines, paid teaching jobs at, and some sort of support for research from, nonuniversity institutions became of extraordinary importance for aspiring sociologists. In the interwar period, the most suitable teaching institution for sociology outside the universities was the Free School of Political Sciences in Prague, founded by the Czechoslovak Ministry of Education in 1928 as a post-secondary establishment which provided 2 years-long training in social sciences and journalism. Sociology was one of the central subjects on the school's curriculum, with Chalupný as its professor and a dozen other sociologists teaching various courses; the school also generated rare teaching opportunities for academics specializing in other social sciences that lacked even the degree of official recognition accorded to sociology: political science, international relations, public administration, or social policy (Hoffmannová 2009, p. 220; Nešpor 2011, pp. 54–56).

Some sociological research was carried out under the auspices of the Social Institute of the Czechoslovak Republic, an advisory body to the Ministry of Social Welfare established in 1920, with which virtually everyone interested in sociology had an honorary affiliation (Rákosník 2007). In the late 1920s, when the Rockefeller Foundation went looking for an academic partner in Czechoslovakia with which to cooperate in the social sciences, its representatives chose the Social Institute over any of the country's universities upon the recommendation of their Czech interlocutors (among them Alice Masaryk), who felt that the conditions at the institute were more suitable for the type of empirical work the foundation was interested in supporting. But even the Social Institute was permanently short of funds, and since its primary task was to provide expert advice in practical questions of social policy, the support it could give to sociology and social research was fairly limited.

The first professional association of Czechoslovak sociologists, the Masaryk Sociological Society (MSS), was founded in 1925 with essential assistance from the Social Institute, which provided office space, clerical support, and a modest yearly contribution (sharply reduced in the wake of the Depression). Ten years into the society's existence, its president Chalupný complained that 'the MSS has never had and still does not have a material endowment that would be even remotely sufficient for any research or publication activities' (Chalupný 1935, p. 89). The society's agenda was reduced to organizing public lectures and sponsoring a book series in which original or translated sociological works were published, if and when the financial situation permitted. While it held regular business meetings, no national conference was ever organized, perhaps due to the small size and hierarchical character of the national sociological community. The society was controlled by a narrow disciplinary elite consisting of university professors, docents, and their chosen assistants; its other members were sociological amateurs recruited mostly from the ranks of public servants, academics from related fields, and students (who set up their own section). At the end of 1931, the membership body was composed of 48 regular members and 80 affiliated members, many of them students, and the average rate of growth in membership until WWII was just above 10 new members every year. In 1934, the newly created title of a 'corresponding member' was awarded to 59 foreign, mostly American or Western European sociologists, including Charles Ellwood and Pitirim Sorokin (Chalupný 1935; Zelenka [1941] 1992).

The Masaryk Sociological Society did not remain immune to the tensions within the disciplinary elite. In 1930, when substantive differences and personality issues erupted in an open conflict between Chalupný (who allied himself with the Brno group around Bláha) and the Prague group led by Král, the Prague fraction decided to leave the ranks of the society and found their own. They did so officially several years later in 1937 when the Society for Social Research was established by members and affiliates of the Prague sociological seminar with the express goal to promote 'social scientific research based on empirical and objective methods' (Machotka et al. 1937, p. 332). This motto meant by implication that, in the eyes of the secessionists, the type of sociology cultivated within the Masaryk Sociological Society was philosophical or journalistic rather than scientific. The Prague group's conviction that Chalupný and his allies in the MSS, Bláha among them, represented an obsolete form of sociology was the main reason for the society's disintegration and also an essential factor that contributed to Czechoslovakia having not just one but two sociological journals.

Before the arrival of specialist sociological journals, Czech sociologists published their articles mostly in the philosophical and general interest periodicals founded by Masaryk and his followers, such as *Naše doba* (*Our Time*) or *Česká mysl* (*Czech Thought*). The first truly sociological journal, *Sociologická revue* (*Sociological Review*), was launched by Bláha in 1930 and soon became the official journal of the Masaryk Sociological Society. Bláha and the members of his sociological seminar in Brno held the editorship of the journal for the entire duration of its existence, which closely copied the democratic era in Czechoslovakia (1930–1940, 1946–1949). In addition to articles by Czech and foreign authors (among them Sorokin, Eubank, Robert MacIver, or Robert Michels), the journal featured a huge review section in which hundreds of new books and journals, both national and foreign, were reviewed every year, further proof of the seriousness with which Bláha worked to make Czech sociology part of the international sociological dialogue. The second journal, *Sociální problémy* (*Social Problems*), was established a year later, in 1931, by the rival Prague group as a part of its strategy to cultivate 'collaboration among the individual social sciences on a sociological basis for the sake of the objective and unified study of society and genuine cooperation between theory and practice … aiming at the purposeful alteration of the social order' (Editors 1931, p. 2). This journal appeared less frequently and its book review section was much less comprehensive, but it equaled its rival as far as the quality of the published articles was concerned. It should be noted that both groups used their journal to print devastating attacks on the published work of their opponents (Nešpor 2011, *passim*).

'Objectivist' Empirical Sociology, Its Proponents and Antagonists

The existence of two sociological associations and two journals testified to a deep split in the Czech sociological community in the interwar period. It is worth stressing again that this dualism reflected a fundamental substantive tension in Czech sociology rather than merely a rivalry between two geographical centers, Prague and Brno. At the heart of it was the conflict between a small group of younger sociologists from the Prague group, intent on practicing sociology as they had encountered it in the most advanced Western centers, and the adherents of the more traditional version of sociology, derived in the last instance from

Masaryk. The two most accomplished proponents of the 'Western' conception of sociology, Zdeněk Ullrich, and Otakar Machotka, had spent some time studying at various universities in Germany and France. There they absorbed new theoretical and methodological ideas which they were determined to inject into Czech sociology.

Zdeněk Ullrich (1901–1955), whom Heinz Maus in his bird's eye survey of Czechoslovak sociology (1962, p. 171) called 'very promising' in retrospect, was interested in a broad range of topics from historical and empirical sociology. His main contribution to the field consisted in a series of empirical research projects, the most important of which was a collective study of the urbanization of the rural or semirural communities surrounding Prague, undertaken in 1932–1934 with a grant from the Rockefeller Foundation (Janišová 1998, p. 36). The project resulted in a book, *Sociological studies on the urbanization of the surroundings of Prague* (Ullrich et al. 1938), of which Ullrich was the editor and the main author, responsible, among other chapters, for the methodology and conclusions. The research drew on official statistics as well as on the data collected by members of the sociological seminar at Prague's university. It has been argued that the book is one of the first applications of the Chicago School's ideas on an European city (Musil 2012, p. 411).

Otakar Machotka (1899–1970) was also one of the contributors to the study of the urbanization processes in the Prague area. Like Ullrich (as documented in their jointly written manifesto *Sociology in modern life*), he was a supporter of scientific sociology based on an 'exact objective method' (Machotka and Ullrich 1928, p. 34), by which they meant above all empirical research producing knowledge that could be put into the service of social and political reform. Machotka had the opportunity to familiarize himself with the latest research methods during his Rockefeller fellowship at the Universities of Chicago and Southern California in 1934–1935. The empiricist credo dominated Machotka's work in the early stage of his career, which reached its peak with his central role in the social survey of the housing conditions of the poor in Prague (published as *Families in social need*, Machotka 1936).

It was the political sociologist Jan Mertl (1904–1978), another member of the younger cohort, who triggered a dispute between the adherents of scientific empirical sociology and the older generation who defended the broad conception of the discipline derived from Masaryk. In his pioneering book on political parties, Mertl (1931, p. 3) paid homage to Max Weber, pugnaciously declaring the 'positive, empirical, and value-free method' to be 'the only correct and fruitful method of sociological research.' The Masarykians were outraged, and a short war of method known as the 'objectivism debate' ensued (1931–1932) (Kilias 2001). The most sustained resistance to the discipline's reorientation came from Vasil K. Škrach, the personal secretary to Masaryk. Škrach's views deserve some attention, as they have the virtue of bringing to light in crass terms the rift between the followers of Masaryk, who considered sociology to be a sort of enlightened public activism that connected philosophy with political practice, and the partisans of sociology as an empirical science:

> There is no more perilous theory in this [present] situation of crisis, under this pressing necessity to take decisions, than sociological objectivism ... It appears that some people want to break with the tradition of our Masarykian sociology, which is anti-objectivist, dynamic, historical, practical and reformist in its orientation, and that they crave for a sociology that is de-philosophized, de-historicized, 'exact', 'empirical', disengaged, impersonal, value-free, de-ideologized ... (Škrach 1932, p. 218)

Škrach went on to identify the foreign influences responsible for the rise of this dangerous 'superficial positivism,' 'without faith, without ideology': First there was Durkheim, then Weber, but less Weber himself than his interpreters, and also German formal sociology (ibid.). It is striking that he made no mention of what was to become the most powerful source of objectivist ideas, US-American empirical sociology. This omission may have resulted from the fact that most things American enjoyed a high level of prestige among the elite of interwar Czechoslovakia, and associating one's opponents with American sociology would not have served the criticism well; or perhaps it was because the influence of the new American research methods was not yet visible within Czech sociology. In any case, Škrach's critical effusion demonstrates that the followers and epigones of Masaryk were not willing to cede an inch in their determinedly anti-scientist vision of sociology. Their camp was very influential in the interwar public discourse, and the resulting intellectual climate had a more fatally limiting effect on the development of 'objectivist' sociology than the lack of resources mentioned earlier.

The academic careers of Machotka and Ullrich, who were still by far the two most successful members of the younger cohort in Prague, are evidence of the obstacles that stood in the way of aspiring academic sociologists in inter- and post-war Czechoslovakia. Both were fortunate enough to find permanent employment in research-related jobs close to sociology at the State Statistical Office; from 1927, Ullrich was also the only (unpaid) assistant in the sociological seminar at Prague's Faculty of Arts. But their effort to give empirical sociology a firm grounding and to build the required research infrastructure proved to be an upward battle. The attempts in the 1930s to set up a sociological research institute either at the Faculty of Arts (Nešpor 2014, p. 137) or at the Social Institute were futile. By the end of the decade, the time was still not ripe for empirical sociology's ascension to a position of academic acceptance anywhere in Czechoslovakia. Even the greatest pessimist could not have predicted that the next opportunity would not present itself until more than half a century later.

Machotka received his habilitation quite early (in 1933), but in Bratislava, and he had to wait until 1946 for his professorship at Prague's university. Ullrich became a docent in Prague in 1937, but his professorship, awarded also in 1946, was at the newly established School of Political and Social Sciences, which was separate from Charles University. The bitter irony was that Machotka and Ullrich became professors only 2 years before sociology in Czechoslovakia was abolished by the communist government.

Elimination in Two Stages (1939–1945 and 1945–1950)

In the Czech literature, the years 1945–1950 are treated either as a postlude to the history of interwar sociology or as a prelude to the discipline's development during communist rule (1948–1989) (Nešpor 2011; cf. Voříšek 2012). If the former approach has been adopted here, it is because of the far-reaching personal, institutional and intellectual continuities with the pre-WWII period. It is worth noting, however, that the academic trajectories of the main protagonists of 1960s Marxist sociology had their origins precisely in the years preceding the February 1948 coup that turned Czechoslovakia into a Stalinist dictatorship. The years 1945–1950 are a transitional period in which interwar Czech sociology, whose main figures were of a socialist but not Marxist political orientation, saw itself increasingly confronted, and eventually replaced, by Marxist-Leninist philosophical doctrine. The extent to which all traces of the old sociology were erased from academic life was such that when sociology made a comeback to Czechoslovakia in the 1960s, it was characterized by a radical disconnection from its 'bourgeois' predecessor (Voříšek 2012, p. 76).

In the 6 years of the Nazi occupation (1939–1945), Czech sociology was devastated by the closure of all institutions of higher education, the policies of extermination of Jews and other minority groups, the brutal persecution of the resistance, and censorship. The type of sociology practiced under the German 'Protectorate' was very much the old interwar sociology, but in the prevailing circumstances no work of outstanding quality was produced (Nešpor 2014, pp. 142–143). Whereas university teachers were forced into retirement or dismissed, those employed in the civil service were often able to keep their jobs. Collaboration with the Nazis was rare among sociologists, most of them were devoted supporters of the First Republic and remained more or less close to its Masarykian spirit. The two journals suspended their publication, but the Sociological Society continued to operate after removing Masaryk's name from its official title. Sociology became attractive for a number of left-wing young people, who even received some sort of sociological training under the auspices of the association. When the war ended, they joined the Communist Party and soon would play a role in the discipline's abolition (see Císař 2005, pp. 157–161).

Liberation in 1945 inaugurated a new system of limited democracy (called, in the common parlance of the day, 'people's democracy') with strong nationalist and socialist accents. Only four political parties were allowed in the Czech political system, three of them leftist (the National Socialists,[4] the Social Democrats, and the Communists). The Communist Party, which could rely on strong backing from Moscow, was unstoppable in its ambition to seize all political power in the country for itself. At the same time, the country's big political issues, such as special ties with Joseph Stalin's Soviet Union, extensive socialization of capitalist industry, and post-war retributions and ethnic cleansings, were widely supported across the entire political spectrum. Intellectuals, sociologists included, were for the most part fascinated by what seemed to be the promise of a new and better society. The outcome of this political fermentation of 1945–1948, and intellectuals' ambivalent contribution to it, was aptly summarized by Bradley Abrams as:

> ... a large-scale swing in Czech cultural self-consciousness away from historic ties to the West and toward the Slavic and socialist East. The Czech intellectual caste presided over this, the most fundamental shift in

> self-representation the nation has ever undergone. All political currents, with the partial exception of the Roman Catholic, trumpeted the glories of an ill-defined 'Slavic solidarity' and stood behind President Beneš's plans for a 'new Slavic politics'. (Abrams 2004, p. 281)

Among Czech sociologists, there was no one after 1945 to openly question the new political course which the country had taken; on the contrary, they supported the Czechoslovak national and social 'revolution' (which was led by the sociologist Edvard Beneš as the country's restored president) without any visible reservations. Both sociological journals, restarted in 1946 and 1947, joined the chorus of voices across society in extolling the huge benefits that the new political system was supposed to bring to Czechoslovakia. In the editor's introduction to the first post-war issue of *Sociologická revue*, whose tone was exceptionally pathos-laden even for this author's rather high standards, Arnošt Bláha, calling 'social justice' and 'the national and moral purification' the main tasks of the moment, gave expression to the nation's Messianic mission using language borrowed from Masaryk: 'Our Czech idea is the world's idea. And, once again, it seems without exaggeration that we are marching ahead of the others as regards the speed and genuineness of our organizing in accordance with the principles of social justice…' (Bláha 1946, p. 6). Otakar Machotka was a leader of the May 1945 Prague Uprising against the Nazis and, after the war, he became a high-ranking politician for the Czech National Socialist Party. Not many traces of objectivist sociology can be found in his pamphlet *The socialism of the Czech man*. In it, Machotka took up the basic clichés of Masaryk's philosophy of history in order to present Czech history and the Czech national character as inevitably leading toward a 'lyrical,' 'tenderhearted' form of socialism distinct from Marxism, whose harsh and cold qualities he considered 'alien' to the Czech soul (Machotka 1946, p. 14).

The period after 1945 saw a dynamic institutional development of sociology similar to its expansion after WWI. Teaching was restored at the two sociological seminars (Prague and Brno) almost immediately after the end of the war. Due to the progressivist atmosphere of the time and the widespread belief that the social sciences would provide the guidance necessary for successful social and political reform, two public higher education institutions in the field of social sciences were founded: the School of Political and Social Sciences in Prague (1945) and the School of Social Sciences in Brno (1947). The fact that the social sciences were the principal subjects taught there led the US economist Norman S. Buchanan, who was visiting Prague as a representative of the Rockefeller Foundation in 1947, to comment that the School of Political and Social Sciences was 'a step in the right direction.' He probably was not told that, while the curricula were to some extent inspired by the American social science programs, the appointment of professors followed a strictly political formula that gave the strongest weight to the Communist Party, which promoted communist candidates who taught Marxism-Leninism. Also, the student body was prevailingly communist (Devátá and Olšáková 2010, pp. 160–168; Císař 2005, pp. 160–161).

The following quote from Buchanan's notes from his visit to Prague is indicative of the condition of Czech sociology after 1945:

> Sociology, broadly interpreted, seemed perhaps the most actively cultivated of all the social sciences. There seemed to be more persons in sociology in the younger and middle age groups and they seemed to be working more intensively. This may be partly because the reform measures of the government have a heavy social welfare and social security cast. Partly also, however, the explanation lies in the fact that sociology was less cultivated here than in America before the war. We noted great interest in urbanization problems, problems of the family, rural organization, morale problems, and the like. The government offices also work on sociology problems. Dr. Král, dean of the faculty of letters at Charles University, is the best placed of the university sociologists while the new School of Political and Social Studies also carries on sociology.[5]

The solid presence of sociologists in the 'younger and middle age groups' noted by Buchanan reflects both the agility of the Machotka-Ullrich cohort and the upsurge of interest in the social sciences after the war. But the actual situation was less reassuring. Czech higher education after WWII was in a fluid, almost anarchic state. There were an extremely large number of students, for all those who had been denied university access during the German occupation were allowed to study now. Student 'action committees,' often led by disciplined communist groups, played a prominent role in organizing lectures and even appointing professors. The dictate of students, which some observers called 'studentocracy' or (reflecting the predominantly male composition of the action committees and the young age of the most active members) 'boyocracy,' was at its strongest immediately after the war, but it did not disappear entirely in the subsequent years. After the communist coup of February

1948, it reemerged with increased powers, virtually controlling all Czech universities (Connelly 2000, pp. 100, 105, 187–192). Notorious is the role of the student committees in staging the purges of faculty members and fellow students. The communist students, radicalized by their Marxist–Leninist professors as well as by the powerful Communist Party apparatus, expelled dozens of academics and thousands of students for not being in conformity with the new official ideology. In a sort of a historical paradox, many of these youngish zealots would become the principal agents of the renewal of sociology in the 1960s.

Sociology became the target of political repression immediately after the February coup. The inherent reason for this concentrated attack on the representatives of sociology was related to its very nature: as the study of social structure and social dynamics, it found itself in the difficult position of being a direct competitor to Marxism–Leninism (Musil 2011, p. 393). Machotka and Ullrich were among the first faculty members to be expelled from Charles University. The heads of the sociological seminars in Prague and Brno, Král and Bláha, were sent on forced retirement (receiving from the communist authorities a treatment that was not very different from that by the Nazis 10 years before). Sociology was abolished as an academic discipline in 1950, and the last cohorts of sociology students, if not expelled, were left in a sort of organizational and personal 'vacuum,' finishing their degrees under recently appointed professors in the brand new departments of Marxism-Leninism (Musil 2011, pp. 380, 388).

In the fervent atmosphere of 1945–1950, political agitation and organizational efforts were enormous, but all this left little time for serious research and original theorizing. Czech sociologists repeated and consolidated what they had learned before the war, and worked to catch up with the most recent developments in the West. Before any valuable work could be produced, the coup of 1948 puts a definitive end to interwar Czech sociology. Machotka, Ullrich, and other younger sociologists emigrated. Ullrich succeeded Alfred R. Radcliffe-Brown as the director of the Institute of Sociology and Social Sciences at Alexandria University in Egypt (UNESCO 1952), but he died soon thereafter. Machotka landed in exile in the United States with the assistance of Ernest W. Burgess, whom he had known from the time of his Rockefeller fellowship. The crown prince of the Brno sociological seminar, Antonín Obrdlík—Bláha's son-in-law and like Machotka a Rockefeller fellow in the interwar period—had left Czechoslovakia for a United Nations job in the US before the communist takeover. Edvard Beneš, who unwittingly assisted the communists in their rise to power, resigned from office and died, bitterly disappointed, in September 1948.

Conclusion

Zdeněk R. Nešpor, author of *A republic of sociologists*, the first book-length history of Czech sociology in the interwar period, summed up its international contribution as follows: 'To the question of what pre-Marxist Czech sociology gave to the "world", meaning to sociology on the global scale, the answer can be laconic: (practically) nothing' (Nešpor 2011, p. 240). This judgment may strike the reader as excessively harsh, but it is closer to the truth than any forced attempt at demonstrating the opposite. Nevertheless, in order to do full justice to the Czech sociologists of that period, the extremely hostile political context of their careers should not be ignored. The 'project' in which they participated—the full academic establishment of a new discipline—was truncated by the catastrophe of WWII and its aftermath. It is reasonable to assume that, had it not been for the interference of the Nazi and communist dictatorships, Czech sociology, which had already taken some important steps in that direction, would have been well prepared to integrate into European and international sociology once the cohort born around 1900 arrived in positions of power within the discipline and once the first generation of students trained by this cohort entered into the profession. This counterfactual claim is, of course, just that—a claim. Still, there can be little doubt that continuity with the interwar tradition would have produced a national disciplinary community much more advanced and better suited to contribute to world sociology than the kind of social science that replaced it in the wake of the communist *putsch*.

Notes

1. The years after 1918 saw a rapid expansion of Czechoslovak higher education, one of the crucial components of the state-building process. In 1920, the former Czech branch of Prague's university was declared the rightful successor to the historical university and renamed Charles University; the former German branch was downgraded into a separate German University in Prague. Two new universities were founded in 1919: Masaryk University in Brno and Comenius University in Bratislava

(Hoffmannová 2009, ch. IV.1). Due to the shortage of trained Slovaks, the positions in Bratislava were often taken by Czech academics, many of whom saw this appointment as an interim solution before a better post became available in Prague or Brno. This practice, unsurprisingly resented by the Slovaks, ended with the collapse of Czechoslovakia in 1938 and was not restored after 1945 (see Klimek 2002, p. 457).

2. No chair of sociology existed at the German University in Prague before or after 1918, but several German-language sociologists or social scientists whose interests intersected with sociology spent a portion of their career in Prague, including Max Weber's brother Alfred before WWI and legal scholars Hans Kelsen and Fritz Sander in the interwar period. Sander's ill-timed attempt to set up a chair of sociology at the German University's Faculty of Law in 1938 was unsuccessful.
3. As reported by Machotka and Ullrich (1928, p. 62), some 90 students enrolled for each of Foustka's two sociological seminars in the 1927 winter semester, and the lectures for the broader public organized by the national sociological association under the title 'The Topics of Modern Sociology' had an attendance of 250–300.
4. The Czech National Socialist Party, founded in 1897, had no relation to its German namesake (see Abrams 2004, pp. 61–62). Edvard Beneš had been a prominent member of this party before he was elected Czechoslovak President in 1935.
5. Diary: NSB (Norman S. Buchanan), June 15–21, 1947, Prague, pp. 28–29 (RF, RG 1.1, Series 712 Czechoslovakia, Subseries S, Social Sciences 1947, Box 6, Folder 55; Rockefeller Archive Center, Sleepy Hollow, New York), original emphasis removed.

References

Abrams, Bradley F. 2004. *The struggle for the soul of the nation: Czech culture and the rise of communism*. Lanham, MD: Rowman & Littlefield.

Becker, Howard, and Harry Elmer Barnes. [1938] 1961. *Social thought from lore to science*, vol. 3, 3rd ed. New York: Dover Publications.

Bernard, Luther L., and Jessie S. Bernard. 1933. The European viewpoint in sociology. *Social Forces* 12 (2): 287–289.

Bláha, A. 1946. Přivítání, vděčnost a pocta. Panu presidentovi dr. Edv. Benešovi. (Welcome, gratitude, homage. For President Dr Edv. Beneš). *Sociologická revue* 12 (1): 5–7.

Bláha, Inocenc Arnošt. 1968. *Sociologie*. Prague: Academia.

Chalupný, Emanuel. 1905. *Úvod do sociologie I* (Introduction to sociology I). Prague (privately printed).

Chalupný, Emanuel. 1930. *Précis d'un système de sociologie*. Paris: Marcel Riviére.

Chalupný, Emanuel. 1935. Masarykova sociologická společnost (Masaryk sociological society). *Sociologická revue* 6 (1–2): 79–89.

Císař, Čestmír. 2005. *Paměti: nejen o zákulisí Pražského jara* (Memoirs: Not only of the backstage of the Prague Spring). Prague: SinCon.

Connelly, John. 2000. *Captive university: The sovietization of East German, Czech, and Polish higher education, 1945–1956*. Chapel Hill, NC: University of North Carolina Press.

Devátá, Markéta, and Doubravka Olšáková. 2010. Vysoká škola politických a hospodářských věd, 1949–1953. Počátky marxistického vysokého školství (Higher school of political and economic sciences, 1949–1953. The beginnings of Marxist higher education). In *Vědní koncepce KSČ a její institucionalizace po roce 1948* (The research policy of the Communist Party of Czechoslovakia and its institutionalization after 1948), ed. Markéta Devátá, Doubravka Olšáková, Vítězslav Sommer, and Peter Dinuš, 159–212. Prague: Institute for Contemporary History CAS.

Editors. 1931. K programu revue (On the journal's program). *Sociální problémy* 1 (1): 1–2.

Eubank, Earle Edward. 1936. European and American sociology: Some comparisons. *Social Forces* 15 (2): 147–154.

Hoffmannová, Jaroslava. 2009. *Institucionální zázemí humanitních a sociálních věd v českých zemích v letech 1848–1952* (The institutional base of the humanities and social sciences in the Czech lands in 1848–1952). Prague: Masaryk Institute and the Archives of the CAS.

Janák, Dušan. 2009. *Hodnoty a hodnocení v sociologii Inocence Arnošta Bláhy* (Values and evaluation in Bláha's sociology). Brno: IIPS of Masaryk University.

Janák, Dušan. 2013. Brněnská versus pražská sociologická škola: mýtus a skutečnost (The Brno versus the Prague school of sociology: Myth and reality). *Sociologický časopis/Czech Sociological Review* 49 (4): 577–602.

Janišová, Helena. 1998. *Zděnek Ullrich*. Prague: SLON.

Käsler, Dirk. 1991. *Sociological adventures. Earle Edward Eubank's visits with European sociologists*. New Brunswick, NJ: Transaction Publishers.

Kilias, Jarosław. 2001. 'Socjologia bilansująca' czy 'obiektywizm socjologiczny'? Dwa spory o charakter socjologii czeskiej okresu międzywojennego ('Balance-sheet sociology' or 'sociological objectivism'? Two debates on the character of Czech sociology in the interwar period). *Studia Socjologiczne* 161 (2): 37–66.

Klimek, Antonín. 2002. *Velké dějiny zemí Koruny české XIV, 1929–1938* (Great history of the Lands of the Bohemian Crown XIV, 1929–1938). Prague: Paseka.

Machotka, Otakar. 1936. *Sociálně potřebné rodiny v hlavním městě Praze* (Families in social need in the capital city of Prague). Prague: Orbis.

Machotka, Otakar. 1938. *Americká sociologie: sociální podmínky vzniku a rozvoje* (American sociology: Social conditions of its origins and development). Prague: Melantrich.

Machotka, Otakar. 1946. *Socialism českého člověka* (The socialism of the Czech man). Prague: Czechoslovak National Socialist Party.

Machotka, Otakar, and Zdeněk Ullrich. 1928. *Sociologie v moderním životě: směry, organisace, úkoly* (Sociology in the modern life: Schools, organization, tasks). Prague: Orbis.

Machotka, Otakar, Zdeněk Ullrich, and Josef Král. 1937. Zprávy a poznámky (Reports and notes). *Sociální problémy* 5 (4): 332–336.

Maus, Heinz. 1962. *A short history of sociology*. New York: Philosophical Library.

Mertl, Jan. 1931. *Politické strany: jejich základy a typy v dnešním světě* (Political parties: Their foundations and types in today's world). Prague: Orbis.

Musil, Jiří. 2011. Poslední ročník studentů sociologie po únoru 1948 (The last students of sociology after the 1948 communist take-over in Czechoslovakia). *Lidé města/Urban People* 13 (3): 373–396.

Musil, Jiří. 2012. Chicagská škola a česká sociologie (The Chicago school and Czech sociology). *Lidé města/Urban People* 14 (3): 395–419.

Nešpor, Zdeněk R. 2011. *Republika sociologů. Zlatý věk české sociologie v meziválečném období a krátce po druhé světové válce* (A republic of sociologists. The golden age of Czech sociology in the interwar period and shortly after WWII). Prague: Scriptorium.

Nešpor, Zdeněk R. 2012. Studium a studenti sociologie v Československu před nástupem komunistického režimu (Sociological education and students of sociology in Czechoslovakia before the rise of the communist regime). *Sociologický časopis/Czech Sociological Review* 48 (4): 669–696.

Nešpor, Zdeněk R. 2014. Organizační zázemí akademického života (The organizational base of academic life). In *Dějiny české sociologie* (The history of Czech sociology), ed. Zdeněk R. Nešpor, 121–146. Prague: Academia.

Obrdlíková, Juliana. 1970. I.A. Bláha's federative functionalism. *Sborník prací Filozofické fakulty brněnské univerzity* (Collected papers of the Faculty of Arts, Brno University) G, Řada sociálněvědná 19 (G14), 15–24.

Petráň, Josef. 1983. *Nástin dějin Filozofické fakulty Univerzity Karlovy v Praze* (An outline of the history of the Faculty of Arts of Charles University in Prague). Prague: Charles University.

Petrusek, Miloslav. 2002. Poučení ze zcela nekrizového vývoje české sociologie let 1989–2001 (A lesson from the crisis-free evolution of Czech sociology in 1989–2001). *Sociologický časopis/Czech Sociological Review* 38 (1–2): 7–15.

Rákosník, Jakub. 2007. Sociální ústav 1920–1941. Mozkové centrum československé sociální politiky (Social institute 1920–1941. The brain trust of Czechoslovak social policy). In *Svět historie—historikův svět* (The world of history—The historian's world), ed. Milan Svoboda, 296–316. Liberec: Technická univerzita v Liberci.

Škrach, Vasil K. 1932. Rozhledy po české sociologii (A survey of Czech sociology). *Česká mysl* 28: 218–231.

Ullrich, Zdeněk, et al. 1938. *Soziologische Studien zur Verstädterung der Prager Umgebung*. Prague: Review 'Sociology and Social Problems'.

UNESCO. 1952. Institute of Sociology and Social Sciences, Alexandria University, Egypt. *International Social Science Bulletin: Area Studies* 4 (4): 716–717.

Voráček, Emil. 1999. Emanuel Chalupný, problémy rozvoje sociologie v Československu 20. let a vznik Masarykovy sociologické společnosti (Emanuel Chalupný, the problems related to the development of sociology in 1920s Czechoslovakia and the establishment of Masaryk Sociological Society). In *Emanuel Chalupný, česká kultura, česká sociologie a Tábor* (Emanuel Chalupný, Czech culture, Czech sociology and Tábor), ed. Josef Zumr, 107–130. Prague: Filosofia.

Vořίšek, Michael. 2012. *The reform generation. 1960s Czechoslovak sociology from a comparative perspective*. Prague: Kalich.

Zelenka, Jindřich. [1941] 1992. Přehled (Overview). *Sociologický časopis* 28 (6): 834–840.

CHAPTER 4

1950–1969: Becoming a Counselor to the Socialist Prince

Abstract Following the virulent communist campaign against it, sociology was almost nonexistent in Czechoslovakia between 1950 and 1956. Once a moderate de-Stalinization process started in 1956, sociology reappeared as a subject of some Marxist-Leninist intellectual debates. By 1964, sociology gained a following among disaffected Marxists, and sociological research was widely seen as useful for the country's envisaged economic, social and political reconstruction. The second institutionalization of Czech sociology took place over a short period of time. The Czechoslovak Sociological Association, the Institute of Sociology at the Academy of Sciences and several university departments were all established in 1964–1966. Sociology quickly developed thanks to new international contacts and the support of the Communist reformers. This boom came to an end after the Soviet invasion in 1968.

Keywords Pavel Machonin · Marxist revisionism · Historical materialism Marxist sociology · Prague Spring

On May 27, 1965, the front page of the official daily newspaper of the Communist Party of Czechoslovakia, *Rudé právo* (*Red Law*), featured the same kind of articles as every other day. The opener described at some length the visit of comrade Antonín Novotný, the party's First Secretary and incidentally also the President of the Republic, to Eastern Slovakia. Novotný, the story reported, had a cordial meeting

M. Skovajsa and J. Balon, *Sociology in the Czech Republic*, Sociology Transformed, DOI 10.1057/978-1-137-45027-2_4

with members of the Czechoslovak Youth Union who were close to completing a broad-gauge railway track which was to enable Soviet trains to transport iron ore across the Czechoslovak border without any time-consuming and costly bogie exchange operations. Another article denounced the bombings of the Democratic Republic of Vietnam by 'US-American pirates' and yet another heaped superlative praise on a Prague show by the Alexandrov Red Army choir. Oddly enough, the same front page also featured, under the headline 'The start of a new scientific discipline,' an interview with Professor Miloš Kaláb, director of the recently established Institute of Sociology at the Czechoslovak Academy of Sciences in Prague.

Kaláb, who had made a successful career as an instructor of Marxism-Leninism after 1948, explained that 'Marxism has a pronouncedly sociological character' and regretted that ideological dogmatism and the severance of contacts with Western sociology over the previous 15 years had resulted in the unsatisfactory development of Marxist sociology in Czechoslovakia. Unlike overly speculative forms of historical materialism, sociological research would generate the factual knowledge needed for the country's scientific management while at the same time preserving its footing in Marxist theory, thus making it a well-balanced 'theoretical-empirical science.' Prospects for the growth of Marxist sociology were excellent, he went on to say, for it could draw on the achievements of the discipline of scientific communism, which had evolved from the theory of class struggle into the scientific study of the principles of planning and managing a society that was developing toward communism. Dispelling the interviewer's concern as to whether sociology could produce any results superior to common sense, Kaláb was quick to say that it was enough to read the work of two representatives of American empirical sociology, Paul Lazarsfeld and George Lundberg, to see that sociologists can indeed produce a wealth of important counterintuitive findings (jkd 1965).

In 1948, sociology had been declared a bourgeois pseudo-science that served the interests of capitalism and was banned forever from academic and intellectual life. Fifteen years later, it made a triumphant comeback, and its American representatives were praised on the pages of *Rudé právo*. This chapter will attempt to clarify how this change came about, but also what kind of discipline eventually emerged out of the alliance between Marxism-Leninism and sociology.

1950–1964: The Existence of a Nonexistent Discipline

In the early years of the 1950s, Czech sociology was ousted from the universities, the publication of its journals discontinued, its academic representatives silenced or exiled, students dispersed. Chalupný and Bláha's desperate attempts at striking a compromise with Marxism-Leninism were met with cold indifference on the part of the representatives of the new regime (Connelly 2000, p. 131; Voříšek 2012, pp. 96–105). The founder of the Czech sociological tradition, Tomáš G. Masaryk, became the target of the most vicious public campaign, and his books disappeared from circulation. Direct political persecution was an exception among sociologists, but the potentiality of it, tied with the gravest personal consequences, was omnipresent.

Even though it was now officially extinct, sociology continued to be bullied by the fanaticized adherents of Marxism-Leninism. One particularly virulent critic denounced the empirical research on the working class conducted at the Czechoslovak Institute of Work around 1950 for using 'the theory and method of reactionary American bourgeois sociology.' Because they asked workers 'unimportant' questions, for instance, about their grandfather's profession, instead of 'important' questions concerning their involvement in socialist shock brigades, the criticized authors were accused of having missed 'lawlike, decisive, intrinsic and organic connections' by focusing on 'minor facts' (Sochor 1951). No less destructive than this defamatory campaign was the frequent harassment of members of the former academic elite by the authorities; coupled with the disorganized nature of public life and economic shortages, the conditions were extremely unpropitious even for intellectual work in private seclusion, not to mention regular employment at an official academic institution.

But sociology remained extinct for a much shorter time than might be suggested by the fervor with which it was abolished. The deaths of Joseph Stalin and his Czechoslovak epigone Klement Gottwald in 1953 put an end to the most acute totalitarian period. The de-Stalinization process initiated at the 20th Congress of the Communist Party of the Soviet Union in 1956 resonated strongly across the Soviet satellite states, producing in the intellectual sphere the phenomenon of Marxist 'revisionism' (Kopeček 2009). Czechoslovakia did not see the same kind of political upheavals that shook Hungary and transformed Poland, but a brief period of liberalization changed the Czechoslovak intellectual climate as well. Things were in motion again, most of the time under the surface, but sometimes erupting in politicized 'affairs' that involved academics who fell into disgrace with the party (Urbánek 1970, p. 131; Devátá and Olšáková 2010, pp. 85–89).

While the 1950s were clearly a lost time for sociology, it should be noted that during this decade the frenzied organizational activities of the Communist Party created a new institutional matrix within which Czech sociology would be reestablished a few years later. This matrix consisted of three types of institutions: research institutes at the Academy of Sciences, university departments, and professional research institutes sponsored by various ministries of the Czechoslovak government.

At the peak of Stalinism in 1952 the communist authorities established a giant centralized research institution, the Czechoslovak Academy of Sciences, in an effort to fully align themselves with the Soviet academic model. Yet, the Academy's establishment happened in parallel not only with the Soviet-style reorganization of research in other communist-bloc countries, but also with the massive increase in public research funding in the West after 1945 (Backhouse and Fontaine 2010, p. 192). The Academy quickly expanded in size until, in 1969, it encompassed 138 research institutes and other research centers and had over 13,000 employees throughout Czechoslovakia (Winters 1994, pp. 282–284). Even though social sciences and the humanities benefited greatly from this development, which gave them a new institutional basis, the strict ideological control over all research at the Academy was especially damaging for these disciplines.

The Czechoslovak system of higher education was overhauled several times in the 1950s, but its shape at the end of the decade remained mostly unchanged until 1989, and in some respects until today. Palacký University in Olomouc had been founded in the previous decade (1946), and now the 1950s saw the establishment of, among others, the Higher School[1] of Economics, the Higher Party School of the Central Committee of the Communist Party, and the Military Political Academy, all of them set up in 1953 and based in Prague (Urbášek and Pulec 2012, pp. 204–205, 222–224). One of the most consequential innovations introduced into Czechoslovak universities after 1948 was the adoption of the Soviet system of university departments (*katedry*) which replaced the traditional chairs held by individual professors. The subordination of these departments to the Ministry of Education was part and parcel of the far-reaching destruction of academic autonomy which affected all aspects of academic life (Pousta 1998, pp. 298–303; Connelly 2000, p. 131).

Professional research institutes attached to various ministries were a third type of institution relevant for sociology. These centers cultivated some form of applied social research in such fields as industrial relations, urban planning, social medicine, or agricultural economics. Since ideological oversight was less intense at this lower end of the academic hierarchy, they became safe havens for those sociologists who were not sympathetic to Marxism-Leninism but wanted to work in a professional position with at least some degree of proximity to sociology (Musil 2004, pp. 587–590).

In a process distantly similar to the pre-WWII situation, the new Marxist sociology in Czechoslovakia after 1956 developed in close connection with philosophy. Unlike sociology, philosophy had not been completely abolished after 1948, but had been transformed into Marxist-Leninist philosophy and a quasi-philosophical discipline called 'dialectical and historical materialism.' After just a few years, both these disciplines had begun to slowly evolve back toward standard philosophy. The bulk of the new personnel at university departments of philosophy and at the prestigious Institute of Philosophy at the Academy of Sciences, founded (first as a 'Cabinet for Philosophy') in 1953, consisted of young people born in the 1920s. Their political outlook, shaped as it was by the extreme experience of WWII, was mostly communist and certainly left-wing. This was the 'reform generation' as Michael Voříšek (2012) called it, which underwent a complicated process of maturation from a naïve faith in Marxist-Leninist ideology after 1945 through various forms of Marxist revisionism during the 1950s to devoted support of the 'democratization process' and 'socialist humanism' in the 1960s. This generation occupied virtually all Marxist-Leninist departments, which in 1957 numbered 68 throughout Czechoslovakia and employed nearly 800 instructors at all levels of the academic hierarchy, 80% of them younger than 35 (Urbášek and Pulec 2012, p. 217).

Toward the end of the 1950s, the fate of sociology across the Eastern bloc began to change for better. In the Soviet Union, the word 'sociology,' if not the discipline itself, was restored legitimacy in the new atmosphere following the 20th Party Congress. In 1956, the first-ever Soviet delegation attended a congress of the International Sociological Association (ISA), held in Amsterdam, and in 1958 the

Soviet Sociological Association was founded (Greenfeld 1988, p. 100). The developments in the Soviet Union were crucially important, since nothing could be done against the will of the party, and the party's will was heavily dependent on the policy shifts taking place in Moscow. But a much more attractive model, the living example of a restored Central European national sociology, was provided by neighboring Poland, where sociology was 'pardoned' in 1956, which led to the resuscitation of sociology programs at the universities, the founding of a national association and Polish sociologists' active role in the ISA (Sułek 2010, p. 329 and *passim*).

In Czechoslovakia, sociology made a renewed appearance as an academic concept as early as 1956 in certain Marxist-Leninist philosophers' debates concerning the nature and tasks of historical materialism. A sort of a new 'protosociology' slowly began to liberate itself from the iron grip of Marxism-Leninism. Paradoxically, this liberation was mediated by highly scholastic exchanges regarding the 'subject and method of historical materialism' and 'scientific communism,' a newly favored discipline after 1956 that reflected the party's sense for the need to analyze contemporary political and social developments in terms of Marxist-Leninist theory (Devátá and Olšáková 2010, p. 90).

In 1956, the official journal for the Marxist-Leninist philosophy, *Filosofický časopis* (*Philosophical Review*), published an article entitled 'On the program for the study of the working environment at large socialist construction projects' (Hochfeld 1956) in which the Polish Marxist theorist Julian Hochfeld outlined the ongoing empirical investigations of working class structure and consciousness in Poland conducted under his tutelage. The fact that empirical social research has been carried out for quite some time in another Soviet bloc country and that Hochfeld, one of the most influential Polish Marxist scholars, was publicly defending its importance presented a weighty argument for those Marxists who wanted to reintroduce empirical sociology into Czechoslovak social sciences. In his commentary on Hochfeld's article, Jaroslav Klofáč, at the time an instructor of historical materialism at the Higher Party School, who would become a central figure in sociology's renewal in the 1960s, wrote:

> Even though there is still no common position concerning the subject and methods of historical materialism, we all concur that without knowledge of concrete social life it is impossible to take any step forward in developing

> social science and overcoming speculativeness and dogmatism. There is no doubt that one important way by which this knowledge of the real life of our society can be attained is by the field research described in the article by Prof. Hochfeld. There is no use in denying that the conditions for sociological research will be more difficult in our country than for our Polish and German comrades. Above all, especially in the beginning, there will be certain personnel issues to deal with, because those working in the area of historical materialism are mostly young and without experience with the techniques of sociological research. It will become necessary to review and reassess the theoretical and methodological premises of Czech bourgeois sociology, the knowledge of which is very scarce in our country, not to say that we know almost nothing about the contemporary state of modern sociology in the West. (Klofáč 1956, p. 449)

This and similar positions adopted in Marxist philosophical writings serve as evidence that sociology was no longer considered completely unacceptable, at least not as a subject of abstract academic discussions. A further sign of the slowly changing official attitude was that before the end of the decade Klofáč—joined by Vojtěch Tlustý, another specialist in historical materialism—was able to publish the book *Contemporary empirical sociology*, a well-informed survey of Western sociological literature which even dared to mention some of the old Czech 'bourgeois' authors (Klofáč and Tlustý 1959).

The turn toward sociology among some Marxist theorists resulted from their frustration with the intractability of historical materialism and scientific communism. Another factor was their realization that the socialist reorganization of society required accurate knowledge of actual social reality rather than ideological phrases and philosophical speculations. But this view was definitely not shared by members of the party apparatus, nor was it accepted by all Marxist pundits. For instance, Ladislav Hrzal and Karel Mácha in their 1961 book *The subject and method of historical materialism* showed some tolerance for empirical social research (thus reflecting the sea change that had taken place in the Soviet Union), but they still saw no need for a new discipline of Marxist sociology and were quite explicit in stating that empirical research must be subordinated to orthodox Marxist-Leninist theory:

> … our surveys of today must have a *class-based* orientation in the sense of their functionality for our form of the dictatorship of the proletariat. (Hrzal and Mácha 1961, p. 106)

In the early 1960s, the proponents of sociology were still far from winning their battle against party ideologues. In the end, it was the subsequent crisis of Czechoslovak socialism that helped sociology to score at least a short-lived victory.

The Impossible Happens: Sociology's Second Institutionalization

The 'protosociological' stage of Czech sociology's revival in the late 1950s was characterized by the continuing dominance of Marxist ideology, but it nevertheless laid the foundations for developments that resulted in the discipline's extremely fast institutionalization in the years 1964–1966. In 1958, a sociological section was established within the national Philosophical Association (*Jednota filosofická*) by certain Marxist philosophers eager to cultivate, following the Soviet and Polish example, a hitherto neglected opportunity for international cooperation. Indeed, the section's main *raison d'être* was to establish working contacts with the ISA. The section's report for the ISA secretariat on Czechoslovak activities in the field of sociology in 1959 shows the inherent difficulty of trying to leave the ISA with the impression that sociological work was going on in the country, while at the same time making it clear to party ideologues that no one saw sociology as a separate discipline from Marxist-Leninist philosophy:

> In the course of this research work, a new methodology of sociological research is being worked out whose basic characteristic is the inseparable unity between direct knowledge of real, actually developing social relations and the deep theoretical approach according to the conception of Marxism-Leninism. The participants of this research do not consider their studies to be a matter of a special empirical science of sociology, but a subject of historical materialism as a scientific discipline which, being Marxist sociology, is simultaneously the materialistic conception of history. Consequently, this concerns a philosophical discipline which considers sociological research to be an auxiliary heuristic discipline.[2] (original English corrected)

Similar precautionary notes declaring sociology to be fully integrated with and subordinated to Marxist-Leninist theory continued to proliferate in official documents and publications well into the second half of the

1960s. But if sociology was to be restored not only as a word, but also as a discipline, the most essential thing to do in a party-ruled state was to convince the party itself of its value. While in the USSR sociology was renewed 'because party officials wanted it' (Greenfeld 1988, p. 102), in Czechoslovakia party officials had to be pushed to want it by academics and functionaries already committed to sociology. This task obviously required superb political credentials and excellent connections within the party's power core. The two most important figures to meet these criteria were Miloš Kaláb and Pavel Machonin, who were both based at the Institute of Marxism-Leninism for Higher Education, an elite institution founded in 1957 in order to continuously improve the qualifications of teachers of Marxism-Leninism at tertiary institutions throughout country (Devátá and Olšáková 2010, pp. 89–95). Although the institute's official mission was to guarantee that the teaching of Marxism-Leninism did not stray from party-imposed orthodoxy and, in particular, to promptly detect and nip in the bud any 'revisionist' inclinations, it soon evolved into a hotbed of reformist ideas. Under Machonin, it later became one of the country's main sociological centers specializing in the research on the social structure of Czechoslovak society.

The reformist tendencies in the Communist Party finally came together in the early 1960s, not in the last instance propelled by the need to find a remedy for Czechoslovakia's ailing economy, which led to the adoption of 'a new system of economic management' and a whole complex of (often vague) ideas concerning the benefits of the scientific steering of society (Skilling 1976, pp. 57–62, 90). This new approach included the notion that it was essential to have empirical data that would not be ideologically pre-fabricated. Empirical social research, and consequently also sociology, thus became increasingly popular not only with the disaffected adepts of scientific communism, but also with reform-minded managers at socialist state organizations and enterprises (Voříšek 2012, pp. 153, 190). Once these considerations gained sufficient support in the upper echelons of the party, the government and the Academy of Sciences, the prospects for sociology's revival improved dramatically.

The breakthrough came in 1964 and 1965.[3] In November 1964, the top management of the Academy of Sciences, the Presidium, approved the guidelines for the Academy's newly established Institute of Sociology, which was officially inaugurated in 1965 with Miloš Kaláb as its first director. Of no less vital importance was the March 1965 decision of the Secretariat of the Party's Central Committee to adopt a report on the development of sociology in Czechoslovakia. The key person in this process of sociology's official rehabilitation was Pavel Machonin, whose role was formalized when he became an influential member of the Academy of Sciences' Academic Collegium for Philosophy and Sociology, the central body overseeing the work done in these disciplines. Also in 1965, a new national journal of sociology, *Sociologický časopis* (*Sociological Review*), was launched under the auspices of the Collegium.

The founding of the Institute of Sociology marked a milestone in the institutionalization of Czech sociology, for this was the first time in its history that Czech sociology could count on a specialized research establishment that was fully funded from the public purse. The Institute's principal research interests were reflected in its division into departments. In 1968, there were departments for: (1) general sociological theory, including the sociology of socialist and capitalist societies, (2) sociological methodology, (3) sociology of work and social groups, (4) sociology of leisure time, (5) theory and sociology of religion. In the same year, the Institute had almost 70 employees and 23 postgraduate students or interns. Sociology seemed to have found its permanent place in the most prestigious national research organization, even though the Institute was located in inadequate premises and its director's requests for the financial resources necessary for further hires were ignored (Voříšek 2012, pp. 241–244).

Two years later, in 1967, the Academy of Sciences set up a small Institute for Public Opinion Research, thus reflecting the growing interest in current opinion on the part of the country's ruling bodies, as well as the public's yearning for democratic empowerment. The first institute of this kind had been created under the Ministry of Information back in 1946, but it was closed down soon after the communist coup (Adamec and Víden̆ 1947; Nešpor et al. 2014, pp. 137, 312). This second attempt to introduce professional opinion polling did not fare much better. Public opinion research was virtually abolished again in the aftermath of the Soviet invasion. However, the short opening of 1967–1969 made it possible for this institute as well as other academic institutions and the media to conduct a number of opinion polls that provide a unique insight into political attitudes during the Prague Spring era (Piekalkiewicz 1972).

The year 1965 marked a breaking point for sociology at Czechoslovak universities. That year, three sociology programs opened in Prague, Brno, and Bratislava. Each was allocated a quota of 15 new students per year, which was exceeded in actual practice. At the Faculty of Arts in Brno, the renewed teaching of sociology in 1965 went hand in hand with the establishment of a new sociology department. In 1966, it grew to include a Laboratory for Social Research and 1 year later it even began to conduct its own public opinion polls in collaboration with the national TV broadcaster (Možný 2004, pp. 610–614). In Prague, although the sociology program at the Faculty of Arts was opened in the 1965/1966 academic year, the department was not established until 1966. The figures reported by department head Eduard Urbánek (1968, pp. 7, 11) for the year 1968 were: 76 daytime students and 40 students in distance learning, three postgraduate students, eight faculty members, one administrative assistant. One of likely purposes of Urbánek's report, however, was to draw attention to the unsatisfactory conditions under which the new department had to operate:

> It is not yet a department in the full sense of the term, since the basic existential conditions for its work have not been secured. Although the situation has improved in this regard, there continues to be a shortage of staff, there are not enough rooms, and there is no technical and material equipment for organizing concrete sociological research. The funding provided for the purchase of sociological literature and journals, especially sociological literature from abroad, is insufficient. … The establishment and construction of the proposed sociological laboratory remains out of sight. The department's activities are also hampered and limited by the fact that various related and auxiliary academic disciplines have not been cultivated at the faculty, such as social psychology, cultural and social anthropology, political science, and management. (Urbánek 1968, pp. 7–8)

In another report, Urbánek vented his frustration at what in his eyes was the disadvantaged status of the universities as compared to the Academy of Sciences—a permanent problem in the dual system of research and teaching that had resulted from the Academy's establishment in the 1950s:

> … the situation of the Sociological Institute of the Academy of Sciences is better and more favorable than that of the Faculties of Philosophy. The Institute has no students and does not organize any training program, and

> yet it has many privileges in comparison with universities and colleges. (Urbánek 1970, p. 140)

Despite these difficulties, in 1969 the number of students in the sociology program at Charles University rose to 200 and at the university in Brno to 140 (Urbánek 1970, p. 131).

A plethora of new sociological departments and centers sprang up at other Czech faculties and universities in the mid-1960s: the Higher School of Economics in Prague, the faculty of journalism in Prague, the medical faculties in Prague and Brno, the faculties of education in Prague and Olomouc, and the technical universities in Prague and Plzeň. Paradoxical as it may seem, in certain respects sociology's development was most advanced at the privileged schools belonging to the party and the military. The department of sociology founded at the Higher Party School in Prague under Jaroslav Klofáč's direction in 1964 was the first in Czechoslovakia, a fact that reflected the School's greater maneuvering space, as it was in fact an organizational unit of the Communist Party itself. Similar prerogatives were enjoyed by the Political Military Academy. It was at these schools that the first translations from Western sociology, including the highly problematic (from a Marxist-Leninist perspective) Max Weber, were published classified as 'internal study materials.' Both schools evolved into important centers of reformist ideas and as such became the victims of the neo-Stalinist backlash following the Soviet invasion.

The Czechoslovak Sociological Association was founded already in 1964. The early supporter of sociology among Marxist-Leninist scholars, Jaroslav Klofáč, was elected its first president. The initiative for its establishment came from the sociological section of the Philosophical Association in 1961, but it took 2 years to break the resistance of the Presidium of the Academy of Sciences, which served as the host organization for academic associations. The constitutive meeting was attended by 400 people, and the total number of members soon reached 1200 (including Slovakia). The association had 13 research committees and six regional organizations. The vast majority of members were, of course, not professional sociologists, as only a tiny fraction could have received some sociological training before 1950. Some data on the composition of the national sociological community can be found in the report from a country-wide consultative conference of Czechoslovak sociologists held in 1966 with the then-president of the ISA, Jan Szczepański from

Poland, as a special guest. Seventy percent of the 450 attendants were aged 30–45 and only 8% declared that they possessed academic training in sociology (Machonin et al. 1966, p. 347; Voříšek 2012, pp. 38–42, 283).

Most of the few surviving representatives of the interwar academic sociology were coopted into the new association, and Josef Král, the head of the former Prague sociological group, was even elected honorary president in autumn 1968, but their role was purely symbolic. The association's leading elite consisted of former Marxist-Leninist academics in their 40s such as Klofáč and Machonin. Politically, the association stood behind the reform program of the Prague Spring. An extraordinary meeting convoked in May 1968, at the peak of the reform wave, publicly declared support for the 'democratization process' and called for further liberal reforms, including the removal of limitations on career advancement for nonparty members. The association sponsored lectures by national and international sociologists and held courses on sociological methods for the public. It was hit hard by the anti-reformist measures adopted with the advent of the 'Normalization' regime after 1968.

The second institutionalization of Czech sociology in the mid-1960s was extraordinarily fast, but it did not come out of the blue. The intellectual and political preconditions for it had been in gestation since the late 1950s. But even though the origins of the revived discipline lay in one particular crisis of the communist system and ideology, sociology's resultant institutional contours have proven to be of a lasting nature. Despite numerous reorganizations and name changes caused by political upheavals, the principal institutions created during the process of sociology's restoration in the 1960s—the university departments in Brno and Prague, the Institute of Sociology at the Academy of Sciences, a national sociological journal, and even the Czechoslovak (later Czech) Sociological Association—have remained at the center of the discipline ever since.

The Relevance of 1960s Czech Sociology

The new level of institutionalization would not have been possible had sociology not gained the favor of an influential segment of Communist Party representatives. That exactly this happened should hardly be taken for granted, since the power of the conservative post-Stalinist fraction, represented by First Secretary Novotný, was seriously threatened only during the short-lived period of political liberalization known as the Prague Spring, stretching from the election of the reformist Communist leader Alexander Dubček as the party's First Secretary in January 1968 until not long after the Soviet invasion on August 21, 1968. The Prague Spring can be described as a failed rebellion of the intellectual elite within and outside the party against the party bureaucrats (see Skilling 1976, pp. 611–613). The recognition of sociology's potential to positively contribute to socialist society was largely the work of the better educated reform-oriented communists, who gradually penetrated into influential positions within the party, the government and the Academy of Sciences. One telling sign of the positive change in the status of sociology and other social sciences was that their representatives were invited to submit official materials to the 13th Party Congress held in 1966. The political engagement of sociologists and other social scientists peaked with their key role in drafting the so-called Action Program of the Communist Party in April 1968, which represented the fundamental political document of the Prague Spring.

When sociology was reconstituted in 1965, its expected official role was to serve as an advisor to a socialist Prince desperate for solutions to serious economic and social problems. In the political polarization leading up to the 1968 events, those most actively involved in sociology's revival found themselves on the side of reform. Responding to the reawakening of Czech civil society, sociology now became 'public sociology' through those of its representatives who were active in media debates and in autonomous civic initiatives. One participant summarized the discipline's roles in the reform movement thus: 'cognitive, critical, diagnostic, and derivatively sociotechnical, but never apologetic' (Lamser 1968, p. 741).

Another major achievement of the 1960s was the reestablishment of contacts with international sociology and with various national sociologies. If the overall conditions for the renewal of sociology in Czechoslovakia after 1956 were much less favorable than in Poland, this was arguably less so because the pre-communist tradition of the discipline was weaker in Czechoslovakia. Instead, the explanation seems to lie in the stricter form of communist government in Czechoslovakia, where all societal autonomy, including the autonomy of the academic sphere, suffered more serious damage than in Poland (Connelly 2000, p. 178). The contrast with Poland was especially sharp when it came to the extent of international contacts tolerated by the regime. Poland, jointly with Hungary, was the Soviet satellite to have the most extensive intellectual exchange with the United States and Western Europe. Especially beneficial for Polish sociology was a Ford Foundation program operating between 1957 and 1961 that provided an opportunity for extended stays at Western academic institutions to some 25 sociologists, including many of those who soon became leaders in their field (Sułek 2010). The fact that the Ford Foundation was unable to start a similar exchange program with Czechoslovakia can be attributed among other factors to the devastatingly high degree to which Czechoslovak academic structures had been colonized by the political power system. As a Ford Foundation observer, John Michael Montias, commented on the situation of Czechoslovak social sciences in general:

> The case of Czechoslovakia is more delicate. There are some outstanding candidates, but it is not clear whether the government would be induced to let them go. Novotný's regime is cordially hated by the great majority of the population; and one may apprehend that some of the recipients might be unwilling to return (although I presume that, as usual, the police would make sure that every recipient had some close family tie to coax him back). From what I know of the personal debasement that accompanies any sort of preferment in this country (and preferment includes travel to the West), we may be fairly sure that any government list would comprise a high percentage of boot-lickers, hacks and sycophants. Still, if a solid agreement could be negotiated, it would be worth trying.[4]

Travel permits to the West continued to be awarded based on political criteria and personal connections well into the 1960s. However, in the second half of the decade restrictions were eased both for outgoing and incoming travel. For sociology, specifically, this development put an end to a long period of isolation from Western academic life. Increasingly frequent were both short conference visits and longer research or study stays abroad. The founding of a regular national sociological association led to a significant increase in contacts with the ISA. In particular, the attendance of more than 40 Czechoslovak participants at the World Congress in Evian in 1966 expanded Czech sociologists' international connections and helped to raise their self-confidence. The lifting of travel restrictions was equally evident in the numbers of visitors. The authorities allowed Czech sociologists to host a number of large international conferences and project meetings, including a 1966 workshop on mathematical methods in sociology chaired by Lazarsfeld. Other prominent visitors included Talcott Parsons, Johan Galtung, Hadley Cantril, Erwin Scheuch, Theodor Adorno, Peter L. Berger, and Pierre Bourdieu. A sort of special relationship developed with Polish sociology. Szczepański and Bauman, among others, attended several conferences, including a large Czechoslovak–Polish meeting held in 1967. Visitors also came from the Soviet Union, other Soviet satellites and—to the dismay of the conservative party ideologists—Yugoslavia, whose special approach to socialism was found attractive by unorthodox Marxists.

One area that is indicative of Czech sociology's international interests in the 1960s is translations. An official report from mid-1960s listed five books that were to be published by the official publishing house of the Academy of Sciences until 1970: Robert K. Merton's *Social theory and social structure*, Lazarsfeld and Morris Rosenberg's *The language of social research*, a reader by Parsons, and one volume each of selected American and French journal articles (Strmiska 1967, p. 510). The fragile nature of the sociological renewal of the 1960s is reflected in the fact that not a single one of these books actually appeared in print. Instead, Czech sociologists avidly consumed books by Polish authors. Until 1970, there were 20 new translations of Polish books, among them four by Bauman. This contrasts markedly with very few translations of Soviet sociology.

Despite this opening to the world, the work produced by Czech sociology in the 1960s was quite limited in terms of its international resonance. Since the bibliometric data for that decade are scarce and unreliable, the most practical way to approach this question is by analyzing the most prominent examples. Following the international trend of setting up large collaborative teams, often spanning various disciplines, several large research teams in the field of social sciences were established in Czechoslovakia in order to address the basic problems of the country's development. Four such teams were founded to investigate the following topics: the economic reform, the reform of the socialist political system, the so-called scientific-technological revolution, and the social structure of Czechoslovak society (Hoppe et al. 2015). The latter two, in particular, were of genuine sociological interest.

The study of 'the social and human implications of the scientific-technological revolution' was begun in 1965 by an interdisciplinary team that eventually comprised 60 social scientists (but only four sociologists). The leader and simultaneously the brain of the project, which received official endorsement from the highest tiers of the party, was the Marxist philosopher Radovan Richta. The team's (and, in the first place,

Richta's) principal achievement was a book, *Civilization at the crossroads*, published in 1966, which was soon translated into several languages. Its principal contention was that the industrial revolution was about to be succeeded by a scientific-technological revolution, the essence of which was that '... there enters into production a far more powerful force of human society—*science as a productive force in its own right*, operating on a basis of all-inclusive social cooperation' (Richta et al. 1969, pp. 27–28). The arrival of fully automated production was set to open new horizons of freedom and creativity for humanity. But, and this was of key importance for the tenor of the book, underlying Richta et al.'s theory was the belief that the expected radical transformation of the productive basis of society with its positive social and human implications could take place only under the conditions of socialism (p. 278).

Richta et al.'s work creatively tailored the concept of the scientific-technological revolution, coined by the British Marxist author J.D. Bernal and later absorbed into official Soviet ideology, to the needs of the Czechoslovak Communist Party in the mid-1960s (Hoppe et al. 2015, p. 49). The Richta team's study was an impressive formulation of a belief in the power of science and socialism to better the human condition, and offered a philosophical rationale for the technocratic reform of the socialist system. With its futurological visions, it struck a deep chord in the techno-optimistic atmosphere of the 1960s. In his book on post-industrial society, Daniel Bell cited extensively from Richta et al., and he later praised Richta as the first sociologist in the Soviet bloc to correctly understand the social consequences of the post-industrial age (Bell [1973] 1999, pp. xxv, 106–112). In retrospect, however, the futurological projections of the Richta study seem little more than a prophecy that was proven wrong by subsequent developments. The central premise of the book, namely that Czechoslovakia was standing at the threshold of a technological revolution, was in stark contrast with the sore state of the country's economy, which was increasingly lagging behind the West. Although Richta et al.'s writing was based on a wealth of empirical material and presented valuable analyses, it was still dominated by the utopian tone inherent to Marxist philosophy. The book supplied abundant bold phrases and vague promises typical of the 1960s Marxist humanism, including talk of a democratization of the planning process and 'socialist participation in advancing civilization' (p. 272), but it did not transcend the narrow vision of the party-controlled scientific management of society.

By contrast, an empiricist concern with actual facts was a paramount feature in the research into social structure of Czechoslovak society conducted under the leadership of Pavel Machonin. This project represented the principal effort of a group of sociologists from various institutions in Prague and Bratislava that had already organized a pioneering conference on the subject of the social structure of socialist society in 1964 attended by Bauman and other leading East European Marxist sociologists. The importance attached to this research by Machonin and his political allies is evident from the fact that the project had the formal endorsement of the Academy of Sciences' Presidium and funding for it had been authorized directly by the Czechoslovak government with approval from the party's Central Committee. The government entrusted the national statistical office with the task of collecting data on a sample of 13,000 male heads of households. The survey was carried out in late 1967, just before the events of the Prague Spring began to unfold. The analytical work suffered delays because of the political engagement of Machonin and other team members. *Československá společnost* (*Czechoslovak society*) was eventually published in Bratislava in late 1969 (Machonin et al. 1969), since at that time Machonin was already on the blacklist in Prague. Nevertheless, the book's distribution was prevented and all copies held by public libraries became 'classified material' until 1989. An English translation was made, but it was never published and only Machonin's summary appeared in the *American Journal of Sociology* (Machonin 1970; this, incidentally, remains the only article by a Czech author in the AJS or ASR since the 1940s).

If there is any monument to Czech sociology of the 1960s, then *Czechoslovak society* certainly is one. From today's perspective, however, the work is full of ambiguities. Machonin et al.'s project was marked by a conscious endeavor to bring Czechoslovak sociological research to hitherto unseen heights of methodological sophistication, motivated by the wish to obtain a truly robust picture of social stratification at home. But their methodological choices were rather idiosyncratic, most likely as a consequence of too short a period of unhampered contacts with international sociology. In hindsight, the project does not compare favorably to the state-of-the-art stratification research then being conducted in the West, as exemplified by Peter M. Blau and Otis Dudley Duncan's 1967 *The American occupational structure*. The analytical framework, however, was complex enough to establish a vigorous research tradition that continues to be a staple of Czech sociology.

The theory of social stratification presented by Machonin et al. was somewhat idiosyncratic, too, but given the circumstances it nevertheless provided an original and bold analysis of a communist society (for a summary, see Voříšek 2012, pp. 213–224). Its centerpiece, a typology of social stratification, showed manifest affinities with the reformist view of recent Czechoslovak history in that it distinguished among the following stratification types which reflected the successive stages in the development of Czechoslovak society: 'capitalist' (until 1948), 'dictatorship of the proletariat' (early 1950s), 'bureaucratic' (Stalinism and post-Stalinism), 'egalitarian' (after 1945), 'technocratic' (1960s), and 'socialist' (corresponding to the normative notion of a 'mature socialism' still to come). In what is only an apparent contradiction, the communist reformer Machonin advocated greater social differentiation in Czechoslovak society,[5] convinced as he was that 'the realistic form of socialism' to be introduced in Czechoslovakia should represent a 'variant of an industrial society, based on achievement and stratified, and consequently differentiated also in interests and views' (Machonin 1970, p. 741; cf. Machonin et al. 1969, p. 165). One of the most astute outside observers of the Prague Spring, Ernest Gellner (1974, p. 172), argued *ex post facto* that by providing the space for interest differentiation, Machonin's meritocratic conception (which Gellner called, with his usual irony, 'anti-leveler') paved the way for the introduction of political pluralism. Abolishing the power monopoly of the Communist Party was, however, a step which even the most progressive Czechoslovak reformers were wary of risking.

Conclusion

The overall balance of the years 1950–1969 is extremely contradictory. On the one hand, sociology was smashed with brutal force soon after the communist regime came to power. On the other hand, the same regime gave research and higher education a new organizational structure that was far broader in scope and more generously funded than anything existing before 1948. This could be considered an important accomplishment, where it not for the extremely oppressive political conditions in which research and teaching developed. It was modernization, but it was modernization *more sovietico*. Once ideological control grew weaker, sociology made a comeback and was allowed to benefit from this powerful institutional dynamism. Yet, again not without a caveat. In the

1960s, sociology operated within a heavy-handed, top-down, centralized academic system that was subordinated and often explicitly subservient to political power. Voříšek has aptly summarized this situation: '… the development of Czechoslovak sociology was directed by the Party, undertaken mainly by Party members and carried out under the auspices of the Party' (2012, p. 29).

Czech sociology of the 1960s attracted some international attention in its time mainly because Czechoslovakia with its reform process was quite fashionable. However, with the partial exception of Machonin et al.'s research on the stratification of Czechoslovak society, Czech sociology did not produce any theories, empirical studies, or methodological innovations of international importance. This is partly due to the fact that the period of the discipline's relatively unfettered productivity lasted less than 5 years. Even more to blame is the restrictive Marxist framework, which sociology not only was not permitted to break out from, but even felt little urge to do so. This limitation was especially evident in the area of sociological theory and theory-based research, where the continued dominance of official Marxist ideas made any truly autonomous thinking, even within the remit of the broader Marxist paradigm, so difficult that very few attempted it and no one succeeded. Paradoxically, given official Marxism's dislike for empirical research, empirical sociology was in a better position to develop under these conditions. But, again, research projects from this period are of little interest due to their descriptive character.

In sum, the most significant accomplishment of 1960s Czech sociology was the establishment of new institutions that have persisted until today. Additionally, the 1960s saw the arrival of modern empirical research informed by sociological theories, methods, and practices from the West and Poland. The period also produced the first handbooks and translations which made international sociological discourse available to Czech students and academics. These factors jointly laid the foundations for the professionalization of Czech sociology in the coming decades.

Notes

1. In Czechoslovakia, the term 'higher school' has denoted a tertiary institution offering mostly professional study programs in a narrowly delimited area. This limited focus and the prevalence of professional training over academic research has distinguished higher schools from universities. Over

time, however, some higher schools have evolved into full-fledged universities while retaining their original official names.

2. Masaryk Institute and Archive of the Czech Academy of Sciences, Public Research Institute, Archive of the Czechoslovak Academy of Sciences, collection Institute of Philosophy (International contacts and cooperation, International Sociological Association, inv. no. 110, sign. 647, box 11, document "I. Institutions and Journals", undated, p. 2).
3. An inventory of sociological centers existing at the end of 1964 lists seven units for sociological theory at universities and the Academy of Sciences, ten centers for specialized sociological research, nine departments of Marxism-Leninism, five research units based at ministries or enterprises, six centers for neighboring disciplines (such as psychology or pedagogics), and the national statistical office—in total, 38 organizational units where some sociological activity was going on (Kohn and Kubecová 1965).
4. Letter from John Michael Montias to Shepard Stone, 18 November 1961 (Ford Foundation records, General correspondence, Czechoslovakia, L60 1193; Rockefeller Archive Center, Sleepy Hollow, New York).
5. One of the main findings of the study by Machonin et al. was that a pronounced 'inconsistency' existed between income on the one hand and complexity of work, education and life-style on the other (Machonin 1970, p. 734). In other words, highly educated individuals (for instance, sociologists) earned less than workers with limited qualifications.

References

Adamec, Čeněk, and Ivan Vídeň. 1947. Polls come to Czechoslovakia. *Public Opinion Quarterly* 11 (4): 548–552.

Backhouse, Roger E., and Philippe Fontaine. 2010. Toward a history of the social sciences. In *The history of the social sciences since 1945*, ed. Roger E. Backhouse and Philippe Fontaine, 184–233. Cambridge: Cambridge University Press.

Bell, Daniel. [1973] 1999. *The coming of post-industrial society.* New York: Basic Books.

Connelly, John. 2000. *Captive university: The sovietization of East German, Czech, and Polish higher education, 1945–1956.* Chapel Hill, NC: University of North Carolina Press.

Devátá, Markéta, and Doubravka Olšáková. 2010. Ideologizace vědy a školství, 1945–1960 (Ideologization of research and education, 1945–1960). In *Vědní koncepce KSČ a její institucionalizace po roce 1948* (The research policy of the Communist Party of Czechoslovakia and its institutionalization after 1948), ed. Markéta Devátá, Doubravka Olšáková, Vítězslav Sommer, and Peter Dinuš, 9–96. Prague: Institute for Contemporary History CAS.

Gellner, Ernest. 1974. The pluralist anti-levellers of Prague. In *Contemporary thought and politics. Selected philosophical themes, vol. II*, 158–174. London: Routledge & Kegan Paul.

Greenfeld, Liah. 1988. Soviet sociology and sociology in the Soviet Union. *Annual Review of Sociology* 14: 99–123.

Hochfeld, Julian. 1956. O programu výzkumu pracovního prostředí na velkých stavbách socialism (On the program for the study of the working environment at large socialist construction projects). *Filosofický časopis* 4 (3): 441–448.

Hoppe, Jiří, Markéta Škodová, Jiří Suk, and Francesco Caccamo. 2015. *'O nový československý model socialismu'* ('For a new Czechoslovak model of socialism'). Prague: Institute of Contemporary History CAS.

Hrzal, Ladislav, and Karel Mácha. 1961. *Předmět a metoda historického materialismu* (The subject and method of historical materialism). Prague: SNPL.

jkd. 1965. Na začátku rozvoje nového vědního oboru (The start of a new scientific discipline). *Rudé právo* 27 May: 1–2.

Klofáč, Jaroslav. 1956. K možnosti a potřebě sociologického výzkumu v ČSR (On the possibility and need of sociological research in Czechoslovakia). *Filosofický časopis* 4 (3): 449–452.

Klofáč, Jaroslav, and Vojtěch Tlustý. 1959. *Současná empirická sociologie* (Contemporary empirical sociology). Prague: Orbis.

Kohn, Pavel, and H. Kubecová. 1965. Příspěvek k vytvoření evidence sociologických pracovišť v ČSSR (Toward creating a directory of sociological centers in the Czechoslovak Socialist Republic). *Sociologický časopis* 1 (3): 336–344.

Kopeček, Michal. 2009. *Hledání ztraceného smyslu revoluce. Zrod a počátky marxistického revizionismu ve střední Evropě 1953–1960* (Quest for the revolution's lost meaning. Origins of the Marxist revisionism in Central Europe, 1953–1960). Prague: Argo.

Lamser, Václav. 1968. Mimořádný sjezd československých sociologů (Extraordinary meeting of Czechoslovak sociologists). *Sociologický časopis* 4 (6): 741.

Machonin, Pavel et al. 1966. I. celostátní porada československých sociologů (The first country-wide consultative meeting of Czechoslovak sociologists). *Sociologický časopis* 3 (3): 347–357.

Machonin, Pavel et al. 1969. *Československá společnost* (Czechoslovak society). Bratislava: Epocha.

Machonin, Pavel. 1970. Social stratification in contemporary Czechoslovakia. *American Journal of Sociology* 75 (5): 725–741.

Možný, Ivo. 2004. Brněnská anomálie? Brněnská sociologie 1963 až 1989 - subjektivní historie (The Brno anomaly? Sociology in Brno 1963–1989, a subjective history). *Sociologický časopis/Czech Sociological Review* 40 (5): 609–622.

Musil, Jiří. 2004. Poznámky o české sociologii za komunistického režimu (Remarks on Czech sociology under the communist regime). *Sociologický časopis/Czech Sociological Review* 40 (5): 573–595.

Nešpor, Zdeněk R. et al. 2014. *Dějiny české sociologie* (The history of Czech sociology). Prague: Academia.

Pousta, Zdeněk. 1998. Univerzita Karlova v letech 1947–1953 (Charles University in 1947–1953). In *Dějiny Univerzity Karlovy IV: 1918–1990*, ed. Jan Havránek and Zdeněk Pousta, 263–305. Prague: Karolinum.

Piekalkiewicz, Jaroslaw. 1972. *Public opinion polling in Czechoslovakia 1968–1969: Results and analysis of surveys conducted during the Dubček era*. New York: Praeger.

Richta, Radovan et al. 1969. *Civilization at the crossroads: Social and human implications of the scientific and technological revolution*. White Plains, NY: International Arts and Sciences Press.

Skilling, H.Gordon. 1976. *Czechoslovakia's interrupted revolution*. Princeton, NJ: Princeton University Press.

Sochor, Lubomír. 1951. Pod vlivem buržoazní sociologie (Under the influence of bourgeois sociology). *Tvorba* 20 (4): 92.

Strmiska, Zdeněk. 1967. II. zpráva o publikační činnosti v oblasti sociologie (2nd report on publication activities in the field of sociology). *Sociologický časopis* 3 (4): 509–510.

Sułek, Antoni. 2010. 'To America!': Polish sociologists in the United States after 1956 and the development of empirical sociology in Poland. *East European Politics & Societies* 24 (3): 327–352.

Urbánek, Eduard. 1968. O znovuzahájení výuky sociologie na Filosofické fakultě KU (On the resumption of sociology courses at Charles University's Faculty of Arts). *Acta Universitatis Carolinae—Philosophica et historica* 4: 5–12.

Urbánek, Eduard. 1970. Sociology in Czechoslovakia. *Social Research* 37 (1): 129–146.

Urbášek, Pavel, and Jiří Pulec. 2012. *Vysokoškolský vzdělávací systém v letech 1945–1969* [Higher education system in 1945–1969]. Olomouc: Palacký University.

Voříšek, Michael. 2012. *The reform generation: 1960s Czechoslovak sociology from a comparative perspective*. Prague: Kalich.

Winters, Stanley B. 1994. Science and politics: The rise and fall of the Czechoslovak Academy of Sciences. *Bohemia* 35: 268–299.

CHAPTER 5

1969–1989: The Long Hour of Party Ideologists

Abstract The neo-Stalinist regime installed in Czechoslovakia after 1968 reintroduced severe ideological control over the social sciences. Most leading figures of 1960s Czech sociology were expelled from the discipline or pushed to the margins. The Communist Party bureaucrats and ideologists who formed the new disciplinary elite subordinated sociology to Marxist–Leninist theory, but also acted to preserve, out of self-interest, the institutions established in the 1960s. Sociology survived both at the Academy of Sciences and in the university departments. While the official sociology was largely inadequate, academic and professional standards could be upheld in empirical and applied social research. The pathologies generated by the oppressive political system, including far-reaching isolation from social sciences in the West, left the discipline with deep academic and moral damage.

Keywords Normalization (Czechoslovakia) · Marxism-Leninism
Marxist sociology · Applied social research · Perestroika

Western sociology today would be unrecognizable without the contribution of the 'disobedient generation' that grew up in the vibrant atmosphere of student protest and cultural experimentation of the 1960s (Sica and Turner 2005). It is a remarkable fact that the 1960s in Czechoslovakia did not produce any influential cohort remotely comparable to the '68 generation of sociologists in the West. This is not

M. Skovajsa and J. Balon, *Sociology in the Czech Republic*, Sociology Transformed, DOI 10.1057/978-1-137-45027-2_5

because young talented people interested in sociology were in short supply at Czechoslovak universities around 1968—on the contrary, a strong new generation was just entering academia toward the end of the decade—but the political oppression introduced after the Soviet intervention in August 1968 had a disastrous effect on their academic careers and often also personal life.

In the aftermath of the invasion, the reformist political program of the Prague Spring was buried by Communist Party hardliners who relied on the coercive power of the Soviet army divisions 'temporarily' stationed on Czechoslovak soil (where they remained until the early 1990s). The terms 'Normalization' and 'consolidation,' which were the two euphemisms used by the pro-Soviet party leadership to refer to the reintroduction of an autocratic system of government, have been adopted in the historical literature to describe the entire period of late communist rule (1969–1989). These innocent terms, in the official language of the day, were intended to hide a massive purge of all those who participated in the reform movement, organized by a regime that was among the most repressive, ideologically conservative, and isolationist in the Soviet bloc (see McDermott 2015, pp. 147–181). The sheer vehemence of the assault against intellectuals, including sociologists, after 1968 led a former committed Stalinist, Louis Aragon, to call the resulting situation 'a Biafra of the spirit' (1968, p. vi).

The neo-Stalinist political establishment that came to dominate Czechoslovakia in 1969 presented, again, a direct threat to the very existence of sociology as an independent discipline. If the scenario of the early 1950s was not repeated, and sociology managed to avoid being abolished altogether, it was not because the actual power holders recognized its worth. The new disciplinary elite was interested in prolonging the existence of a field which they only recently had come to control and which they needed in order to pursue their own academic and political careers. As noted by one observer standing at the margins of official sociology before 1989, 'sociology did not disappear (its institutional structure has been preserved), what did disappear were the sociologists.' (Alan 1988, p. 7) The sociology that was now officially sanctioned was thoroughly a ideologized one, in which unbiased empirical analysis and autonomous construction of theories were replaced by ritualistic citations from Communist Party documents and the classics of Marxism-Leninism. The practitioners of sociology had to face the fact that engagement with actual social reality was one of the central taboos of the existing political system. But even under these adverse conditions the discipline survived, developing semi-official modes of operation on a scale much greater than in the two decades after 1948. Applied research institutes in industry or social and health services provided a relatively safe space for low-ideology empirical research that allowed sociology to remain a form of knowledge engaged with reality and to register some advances on the path of professionalization, especially in the command of quantitative methods and techniques (Musil 2004; Nešpor 2014; Voříšek 2014, pp. 368–376).

The Purge and Its Consequences

'Discontinuity' is the term that imposes itself as the most fitting description of what happened to Czech sociology in the years 1969–1973. This discontinuity was personal as well as substantive. The recently (1965) established Institute of Sociology at the Czechoslovak Academy of Sciences in Prague was closed down as a hotbed of the revisionist epidemic, its director Miloš Kaláb and many other reform-oriented members dismissed or relegated to the lowest ranks of the academic hierarchy. Most of its employees were transferred into the sociological division of the new Institute of Philosophy and Sociology, founded in 1970.

The political vetting which began in the same year targeted first members of the Communist Party and then everyone else (with exceptions being made here and there for the cleaning personnel). The official interpretation of the 1968 reform movement was codified in a document titled 'A lesson from the crisis development in party and society after the 13th party congress,' which was approved by the party's Central Committee at the end of 1970 and frenetically disseminated across the country. According to this document, sociology was one of those academic fields in which reform-minded party members had succumbed to bourgeois ideology and anti-communism. The central protagonist of sociology's 1960s revival, Pavel Machonin, was listed among the most dangerous representatives of the 'right-wing opportunism' within the party. The 'Lesson' specified many other categories of political wrongdoings such as 'revisionism,' 'antisocialism,' 'anti-Sovietism,' 'petit-bourgeois tendencies,' or 'Zionism.'

The cleansing of political enemies at the Institute of Philosophy and Sociology was particularly drastic. The institute-specific party units were dissolved and 72% of the party members lost their membership cards. In total, some 70 employees out of 180 saw their job contracts terminated following a negative decision by the vetting committees (Prokůpek 2002, pp. 206–211). Other disciplinary institutions were also severely affected. Abolition was the unavoidable fate of Charles University's Institute for Political and Social Sciences (formerly the Institute of Marxism-Leninism for Higher Education), where Machonin had organized his research project on the social structure of Czechoslovak society (Machonin et al. 1969). The heads of the sociology departments at the universities in Prague and Brno were replaced, and faculty members known to have sided with the reform movement dismissed or demoted. The admission of new students was interrupted for several years. The only national sociological journal, *Sociologický časopis*, saw its chief editor and most members of the editorial board replaced by party loyalists whose names were not publicly disclosed for several years. A similarly devastating purge swept the Czechoslovak Sociological Association, which lost 50% of its 1969 membership and most members of its governing bodies, including its first two presidents, Jaroslav Klofáč and Josef Solař. Several leading personalities of 1960s sociology emigrated to Western countries.[1]

The break with the past was equally far-reaching in the substantive sense, although it would be more fitting to call it a regression into the proto-sociological stage preceding Czech sociology's revival in the mid-1960s. As Jan Fojtík, the powerful post-1968 secretary of the party's Central Committee, and other party ideologists including those active *within* sociology, never grew tired of repeating, the principal sin of 1960s sociology had been its reluctance to let itself be guided by the true interest of the working class whose only legitimate interpreter was the Communist Party. Reformist sociology had to pay for having 'abandoned the method of historical materialism as the theoretical foundation for the study of social reality' (Fojtík 1972, p. 161). As part of the process of 'consolidation,' sociology again came to be viewed as a discipline whose existence could only be justified by its slavish conformity with Marxist–Leninist philosophy. The notion that the social sciences were directly subordinated to the interests of the party was announced in no ambiguous terms by the former reformist Radovan Richta, who became a central figure in the Normalization process in Czech philosophy and sociology:

> Genuine scientific contribution and true knowledge are made possible precisely because the researcher—philosopher, sociologist—approaches

> reality fully conscious of his actual social (and thus also class) background, because he views himself and his work as a part of the cognitive and practical-critical activity of the Party... It thus follows that the control of research pertains to the party of the working class [*the Communist Party—M.S.*] as the fundamental subjective component of the entire process of understanding and transforming the world. (Richta 1973, p. 339)

With just a handful of exceptions, the group which achieved positions of power in Czech sociology after 1968 consisted of second- or third-rate academics who often were not professional sociologists but Marxist–Leninist philosophers, 'scientific communists,' and party ideologists. Their ascendancy would not have been possible had they not deposed the leading representatives of 1960s sociology and defeated any sense of independence among rank-and-file sociologists during the purges of the early 1970s. To cement their hold on power and prevent any possible revolt, the disciplinary elite had to exercise utmost caution especially when dealing with the younger generation. The positions vacated after the purge were occupied by young academics who either had not been interested in or had lacked the opportunity to sully themselves by becoming involved with the reformers of 1968. Careful personnel selection, in which academic qualities were often much less important than personal loyalty and ideological conformism, guaranteed the security of the discipline's leaders while allowing for generational exchange in the future. It was, in fact, a very distant future, since, except for those who died, Czech sociology's official representatives remained almost unchanged until the collapse of the communist regime in 1989—a situation that closely mirrored the unchangeability of the country's political elites.

This 'frozen' character of the discipline can be shown using several prominent examples. Radovan Richta, the only representative of 'normalized' sociology to enjoy broad international recognition for his work, served as the director of the reorganized Institute of Philosophy and Sociology until his death in 1983. In 1970, an intern at the Institute, František Charvát, was catapulted to the head of the Institute's sociological section at age 30, thanks to his ability to combine mathematics with party ideology. When Charvát's chances to succeed Richta as the Institute's director were thwarted by the appointment of a party *apparatchik*, he moved to Vienna in 1986 to become the director of UNESCO's European Coordination Centre for Research and Documentation in the Social Sciences (as an appointee of the Czechoslovak government). In 1970–1989, the official journal of Czech sociology, *Sociologický časopis*, had only one editor-in-chief, Karel Rychtařík, previously based at the military academy, who combined the job of the journal's editor with that of the director of the Federal Statistical Office's Institute for Public Opinion Research. The most powerful figure in sociology at Charles University in Prague, Antonín Vaněk, served as the head of the university's Institute of Marxism-Leninism (1972–1977), then (1977–1989) as the chair of the sociology department at the Faculty of Arts, and also as this Faculty's dean (1986–1989). This list, which could be expanded to include some, but not too many, other names, is indicative of the extraordinary concentration of disciplinary power in the hands of the very few.

The Pathologies of 'Normalized' Academic Life

The functioning of sociology in its various forms from official to illegal reflected the more general conditions of social life under the Normalization-era regime. The steeply vertical hierarchy of power left the vast majority of the population at the mercy of a narrow elite that relied heavily on the repressive apparatus of police, secret police, and army. Combined with a well-organized system of information-gathering and surveillance, the party's control of, among other things, all employment opportunities, access to educational institutions, and travel abroad gave it immense leverage for pressurizing, blackmailing, and deterring any individual (Šimečka 1984). These instruments of domination, which the representatives of the Normalization regime learnt to handle with extraordinary virtuosity, were also employed within sociology by the new official leaders of the discipline. It is difficult to say with hindsight if their motivation for doing so was predominantly ideological or whether it was mostly self-interested. This dominant group was a collection of very different personal and professional types, including half-educated *apparatchiki*, fanatical ideologists, cynical fellow-travelers, and last, but not least, professionally competent sociologists who, out of a mixture of opportunism and genuine conviction, were able to accept important positions in the new political circumstances. The overall atmosphere was changing. In the early years of Normalization, the party managers of the social sciences were still committed to a notion of sociology representing a genuine development of Marxist–Leninist principles, but in later years the prevailing stance was more pragmatic (or cynical), demanding only outward signs of conformity with ideological prescriptions (Oates-Indruchová 2008, p. 1776).

The Czech sociological community of the Normalization era could be broken down into Communist Party members (to which belonged almost all the representatives of the official disciplinary elite), nonpartisan sociologists and former party members who had fallen into disgrace because of real or fabricated misdeeds against the present regime. In what can be seen as one of the many paradoxes of post-invasion Czechoslovakia, the purges had more devastating consequences for reform-oriented party members than they did for nonmembers. To be sure, those in the latter group had generally been excluded from more important institutional positions since 1948 and remained second-class citizens after 1968, but their lack of political importance protected them from the wrath of the new power holders. The party's treatment of those of its members who were not in conformity with the pro-Soviet line was highly differentiated. The most serious punishment, *expulsion* from the party, usually resulted in dismissal and a permanent ban from academic employment. In contrast, *cancellation* of party membership represented a milder form of disciplinary measure that had as a consequence 'only' the affected individual's relegation to a lower (often temporary) position (Prokůpek 2002; McDermott 2015, p. 157).

The vetting of an individual's political reliability was not just a characteristic of the great purge of the early 1970s; it was a permanent feature of the regime and one of its most deeply ingrained obsessions. Party member vetting, innocently referred to as 'the replacement of membership cards' in order to give the false impression that it was a purely technical procedure, could be repeated at any time, and with grave consequences for individuals not in good standing with the party, as was the case at Charles University in 1979 (see below). No less importantly, political assessments were regularly compiled for every researcher, teacher, and student as a routine part of communist governance, thus providing those in power with repeated opportunities to settle whatever grudges they might have against their colleagues and competitors (Petráň 1998, pp. 461–466). Academic life was organized in a strictly hierarchical manner, whose impact on individuals was amplified by the multiplicity of hierarchies to which everyone was subordinated (Jareš et al. 2012). Academics depended for their professional existence not only on their department heads and deans or directors, but also on the omnipresent

Communist Party units that operated on multiple levels simultaneously (on the departmental, faculty, university, district, city, regional or the national level, but also within the neighborhood of one's residence), and on the relevant local trade union, the Socialist Youth Union, the Czechoslovak–Soviet Friendship Union and other organizations within the spurious public sphere of the authoritarian state. Since authorization from one's superiors in the party and academic structures was necessary for the most basic activities of academic life (teaching and advising students, publishing an article or a book, speaking at a conference at home or abroad, receiving foreign guests, getting a foreign book from the library), there was a widespread feeling of disempowerment vis-à-vis this immense network of decision-makers, controllers, and informers (for a Western view, see Wolchik 2013). The arbitrariness of bureaucratic power went hand in hand with rampant nepotism (Laiferová 2014, p. 21). Children, wives (it may have become clear by now that the power elite was by far mostly masculine), and other relatives or protégés of influential party and academic officials were placed in positions that often exceeded their qualifications and abilities. Nepotism, political interference, and corruption were endemic in the admission of new students as well (Ulč 1978, p. 429).

Another perverse aspect of academic life under Normalization, resulting from the extreme power differential and the corresponding lack of accountability on the part of those in superior positions, was a widespread absence of academic integrity. The standard instruments of academic quality assurance, such as unbiased peer review, were ineffective and purely formal in nature. Perhaps the gravest consequence of the authoritarian organization of the academic field was an unparalleled disrespect for intellectual property rights. Banned authors were forced to publish under pseudonyms or under the names of their acquaintances, if their work could appear in print at all. There were frequent instances of intellectual theft in which well-positioned individuals pretended that texts written by persecuted or less well-connected colleagues were their own (Stehlíková in Konopásek 2000, p. 261). Legal or moral redress in such cases was almost impossible. Economic pressure forced individuals in inferior positions or at the margins of the academic world to write articles, books, or theses for their bosses, for powerful party officials, or for these people's relatives. Often, these same sociologists also carried the burden of undertaking research and writing papers which their more fortunate superiors then read at international conferences which the real authors were not permitted to attend.

These and other pathologies of academic life (and of social and personal life more broadly) during Normalization have been described by Czech and Slovak sociologists in their memoirs and autobiographical analyses (Potůček 1995; Konopásek 2000; Skovajsa 2004). But the picture is still incomplete, as there are no published accounts of Normalization-era sociology from the other side of the divide—that is, from the former disciplinary elite. Also, it is worth noting that sociology's contribution to explaining the peculiar social mechanisms of Czechoslovak Normalization remains rather slim. The most penetrating critical dissections of 'normalized' social life can be found not in sociological studies, but in such works as Václav Havel's 1975 open letter to the President of Czechoslovakia Gustáv Husák (Havel 1992) or Milan Šimečka's chilling description of the system of domination created by the post-1968 regime (Šimečka 1984). By the time sociology eventually made a contribution, as in the *samizdat* journal *Sociologický obzor* (*Sociological Horizon*), published illegally in 1987–1989 by Josef Alan and Miloslav Petrusek, the communist system was already rushing toward its collapse. Normalization and communism more broadly remained a marginal subject of sociological study after 1989 as well, thus validating the observation made by Christian Fleck and Andreas Hess that 'a sociology of communism' worthy of its name has yet to be established (Fleck and Hess 2011, p. 671).

Fields of Sociological Activity

With very rare exceptions, the writings of official Czech sociology in the 1970s and 1980s have found little interest, other than documentary, with Czech readers since 1989, and have received virtually no attention in relevant international discussions. This situation can be attributed to a combination of factors: many competent sociologists were among the victims of the purges following 1968; the potential for original theorizing and research was seriously undermined by the imposition of severe ideological control by the party; certain key representatives of the profession were simply uninterested in providing any original contribution to scholarship; and an academic system built on political conformism did little to promote academic excellence. To this, we should add the far-reaching isolation from developments in the discipline in the West, which was maintained as a part of the system of state control over citizens' lives. While Czechoslovakia was involved in the activities of the International Sociological Association (ISA), or in various research projects sponsored by UNESCO and other international organizations, participation in these was the privilege of a narrow group of official representatives of the discipline. Despite their 20-year monopolistic access to the ISA as Czechoslovak national delegates, the leading figures of Normalization-era sociology never played a role comparable to that of the Polish or Soviet sociologists (see Bucholc 2016, pp. 50–52).

Another important aspect of the Czechoslovak government's policy of keeping the doors to the outside world closed was that the intellectual exchange with the West sponsored by governments or philanthropic foundations was more severely restricted than in neighboring Poland or Hungary. As a consequence, in the 1970s and 1980s the vast majority of Czech sociologists evolved professionally in a situation marked by a minimum of personal contacts with their Western colleagues and fairly limited access to recent Western literature. While the study of theories and methodologies from the West was an established subfield known as 'the critique of bourgeois and anticommunist ideology,' any sympathetic reception of non-Marxist–Leninist approaches remained forbidden until the late 1980s.

The internal reasons for the poor performance of the official Marxist–Leninist sociology in Czechoslovakia can be found in the futile task the party's managers of the social sciences expected it to accomplish. Most fatal for sociology as an empirical and critical science was the pressure placed on it to demonstrate, again and again, that in the clash between official ideology and social reality ideology was always right (Alan 1988, pp. 11–12). The obvious impossibility of this mission went hand in hand with an obsessive effort on the part of official authors to denounce every form of 'incorrect' social thought. The 1970s and 1980s were the heyday of the official defamatory critique, which targeted 'bourgeois' authors from the West as well as Czech and other Soviet-bloc authors who deviated from the official line. Considering the glaring lack of academic competence (displayed, for instance, in treating Vilfredo Pareto as an 'American sociologist'), the scholarly contribution of works such as party ideologist Ladislav Hrzal's hostile assessment of Western sociology was dubious at best (Hrzal 1973; see, p. 42). From a moral point of view, this critique was particularly problematic when it attacked the domestic exponents of 'revisionism' and 'right-wing opportunism' who had been stripped of any means of defense.

The rigid imposition of the official Marxist–Leninist doctrine made any autonomous theoretical thinking, including any sort of 'creative' Marxism, impossible. Likewise, the empirical sociology practiced at the discipline's central institutions (the Academy of Sciences and universities) was subjected to heavy ideological control, censorship and self-censorship. Its preferred topics included social structure and the working class (in an interpretation that was polemically directed against the 1969 book by Machonin et al., see Chap. 4), the socialist way of life, scientific, and technological revolution (a focus that survived the year 1968 along with Richta, but that in the process lost most of its humanist appeal), youth, social planning and forecasting, automatic management systems and other problems of industrial sociology (Petrusek 1988; Voříšek 2014, pp. 362–376). Certain topics could not be investigated, since official ideology ruled out their existence in a socialist society *ex hypothesi* (such as poverty—Večerník 2011).

Sociologists who lacked flawless political credentials, or who were unwilling to make extensive compromises with the ruling ideology, were pushed away from politically loaded topics into more technical and marginal areas of research. In parallel to the elite institutions where ideological conformity was rigidly enforced, a semi-official academic sphere was gradually emerging which constituted an important section of the vast middle ground between the Communist Party and the anti-communist opposition for which the dissident sociologist Jiřina Šiklová (1990) coined the term 'gray zone.' Urban and regional sociology, in particular, provided a protected harbor for non-Marxist sociologists, some of whom (Jiří Musil, Michal Illner) rose to prominence after 1989 (Musil 2004; Szelényi 2012). Empirical sociology could also be practiced with some level of autonomy in applied industrial research, planning and forecasting, health care, sports, and culture. However, this autonomy did not go beyond relatively open discussions, seminars and conferences, and low-circulation publications. Its fragility was repeatedly demonstrated in clashes with party authorities (Nešpor 2014, pp. 123–126). One particularly subversive research unit based at the state socialist company Sportpropag[2]—whose collaborators included Machonin and other banned sociologists—had to be quickly dissolved in 1983 after a conference volume it had published came to the attention of the Central Committee (see Kabele 2011).

The retreat into applied social research was an effective defense mechanism, under the given circumstances, but it could not prevent a far-reaching degradation of the discipline. The most common reaction to the all-pervasive ideological surveillance among Czech sociologists from the official and semi-official sphere was a turn away from any form of theoretical framing toward plain empiricism and 'sociotechnical' applications. Social research could develop relatively unhampered by political dictates, provided that the research topics were sufficiently insignificant and narrowly delimited so as not to provoke any suspicions within the party. Methodology became possibly the largest domain within Czech sociology, since it presented the easiest way to avoid the real social problems and pathologies of the Normalization era. But as Petrusek noted in his scathing critique of the state of the discipline in the late 1980s, much methodological work was strictly technical and outdated when compared to the international state of the art (Petrusek 1988, p. 30).

The devastating effects of direct political control were particularly strongly felt in the public opinion polling conducted at the Institute for Public Opinion Research (which survived several reorganizations in the early 1970s) and at several other academic centers such as the party's Higher School of Politics (formerly the Higher Party School, renamed, and thoroughly cleansed of 'opportunist' elements after 1968). Even though opinion surveys often concerned important issues (including the population's awareness of the Chernobyl disaster in 1986), the reports containing full information and analyses were strictly classified materials available only to the authorized personnel of the Central Committee. If any studies based on public opinion data were published in academic journals at all, they were stripped of all sensitive information and strictly followed the official party line (Šiklová 1988).

The re-ideologization of Czech sociology and its isolation from Western literature under Normalization can be illustrated using data from *Sociologický časopis*. As shown in Fig. 5.1, the eponymous founders of Marxism–Leninism were invoked much more frequently in the two decades of Normalization than ever before or after. Lenin's authority was most heavily exploited right after 1969, when sociology's survival was far from certain and quoting Lenin meant playing it safe in relation to both the Soviet and the national party authorities. Marx's name appeared consistently less often than Lenin's during most of Normalization, but Marx's presence proved to be more resistant to decline in the final years before 1989.

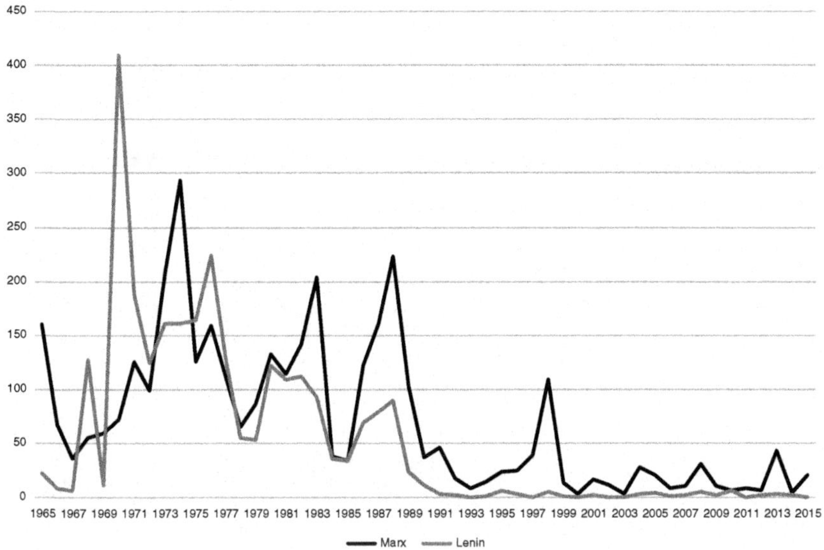

Fig. 5.1 Frequency of occurrence of the terms 'Marx' and 'Lenin' in *Sociologický časopis/Czech Sociological Review*, 1965–2015. *Note* based on a full-text search of the journal

An inverse development can be observed when it comes to influences from the West. Figure 5.2 shows the average number of references in *Sociologický časopis* to the three 'core' US-American journals (i.e., ASR, AJS, and *Social Forces*—Allen 1990) by 6-year periods. The data indicate that, especially between the mid-1970s and the mid-1980s, references to US journals were very scarce—less common than in the liberal 1960s and much less frequent than in the post-communist period. On the whole, the official journal of Czech sociology displayed the same kind of behavior regarding references and citations as revealed by Ivan Dianiška's critical assessment of its Slovak counterpart, *Sociológia* (Dianiška 1989). This pattern can be summarized as follows: a sharp drop in the number of references to Western sociological literature after 1969, complemented by an equally brusque increase in the number of references to publications from the Soviet bloc, especially the Soviet Union itself; a clear focus on the national literature; high, though oscillating levels of references to classical Marxist–Leninist authors; similarly cyclical reference frequencies for Communist Party documents, which reach a peak

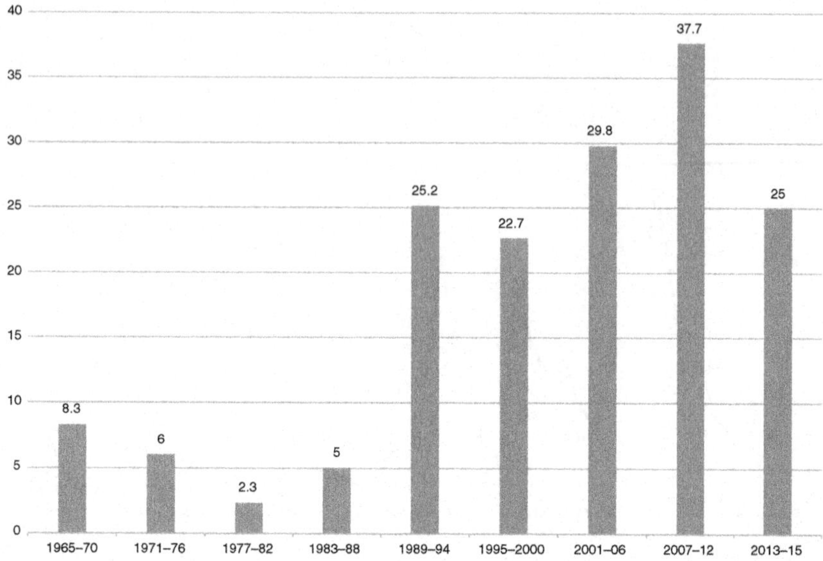

Fig. 5.2 Yearly average numbers of references to core US journals in *Sociologický časopis/Czech Sociological Review*, 1965–2015, per 6-year periods. *Note* data for 1965–2003 from a full-text search of the journal, for 2004–2015 from Journal Citation Reports, Web of Science (accessed on Dec 17, 2016)

every 5 years in a rhythm determined by the schedule of the party congresses; and sparse references to pre-1948 and 1960s national sociology.

The Reproduction of Sociology at Universities and Within the National Association

The Normalization-era regime was quick to close down university departments that it perceived as incompatible with the official party line. All departments of Marxism–Leninism, polluted as they had been by the 1960s revisionist thinking, were disbanded and replaced by new Institutes of Marxism–Leninism controlled by pro-Soviet loyalists. The departments of sociology in Prague and Brno, which had been the only places where students could receive training in something resembling standard academic sociology, were abolished in 1971. Politically unacceptable staff were dismissed and the rest transferred to the newly created departments of Marxist–Leninist philosophy. At the Faculty of Arts in Prague, sociology was subsumed under this department's division for scientific communism and social research, which existed next to the divisions for dialectical and historical materialism, the history of philosophy, logic, and political economy. The division for scientific communism was soon renamed back into the division for sociology, but the situation deteriorated again in the second half of the 1970s. Both the study program and the department (which was reestablished in 1977) were rebranded as 'Marxist–Leninist sociology.' The quasi-obligatory requirement that the teaching staff be members of the Communist Party, coupled with a new wave of political vetting, led to the dismissal of several department members, among them the future dean of Charles University's post-1989 Faculty of Social Sciences, Miloslav Petrusek (Urbánek 1994, p. 86; Petrusek 2004, pp. 603–605). Extremely tight party control over the Faculty of Arts ensured that the study of sociology in Prague prior to 1989 remained highly ideologized. Nevertheless, the study program at Czechoslovakia's most prestigious school for humanities and the social sciences at the time continued to be attractive for students, many of whom later became lifetime professional sociologists. From 1977 to 1984, 184 students graduated from Charles University's sociology program, an average of 26 every year, including 10% foreign nationals (Duffková 1985, p. 427).

Developments in Brno resembled those in the capital, except that the degree of ideological control (and also the professional qualifications and personal characteristics of the individuals in leadership positions) was more favorable to sociology's survival as a standard academic discipline. In 1971, when sociology was made merely a division in the department of Marxist–Leninist philosophy, politically 'unreliable' faculty members, including the future founding dean of Brno's Faculty of Social Studies in 1998, Ivo Možný, were transferred to the affiliated Laboratory for Social Research (see Chap. 4) and were banned from teaching and publishing. The division was not upgraded into a department of Marxist–Leninist sociology until 1980. The slow but steady easing of restrictions on academic work resulted in a gradual resumption of genuine sociological activities and the recruitment of promising younger instructors in the 1980s; these factors gave Brno a competitive advantage over Prague in the period after 1989 (Možný 2004, pp. 614–621).

In the first years after the onset of Normalization, when it was not clear whether sociology would be allowed to exist, no new students were admitted to the sociology programs in Prague and Brno, and it was not until 1973 that first-year students were admitted again.[3] The curriculum had a heavy ideological bias which left only limited space for sociological courses. According to the head of the Prague department, Antonín Vaněk, starting from 1978 the sociological curriculum was the same for all three Czechoslovak departments (two Czech, one Slovak in Bratislava), and consisted of four segments:

1. Core courses required for all study programs, including the history of the Czechoslovak Communist Party and the international working-class movement, Marxist–Leninist philosophy, scientific communism, scientific atheism, and Russian (a total of 1215 teaching hours);
2. Supplementary courses such as a second (Western) language, political service, sports, and civic defense (405 teaching hours plus another 600 hours of military training for male students); the only remotely sociological course in this group was industrial field research;
3. Program-specific courses which combined ideological subjects such as Marxist–Leninist sociological theory or a critique of bourgeois sociology and anticommunism with more standard offerings such as the history of social theory, the history of Czech sociology, the social structure of Czechoslovak society, mathematics, statistics, and methodology (1320 teaching hours);
4. Specialized subjects ranging from the favored sociology of work and industrial sociology to courses on the socialist lifestyle, family, and youth, or other frequent topics of official sociology (840 teaching hours) (Vaněk 1980, pp. 251–252). Even according to the most optimistic estimate, no more than 50% of all courses in the curriculum were directly relevant to sociology.

The extent to which the aims of new sociologists' professional training were subordinated to the ideological agenda of the Communist Party can be seen in Vaněk's description of the model graduate that the sociology program was expected to produce:

> Graduates must gain a profound and full command of the theory of Marxism-Leninism in all its component parts, in particular the Marxist

> theory of social development; they must adopt and rationally and emotionally internalize the scientific worldview, and they must perfectly master the methodology of studying social phenomena on the basis of the study of the classics of Marxism-Leninism, the documents of the Central Committee of the Communist Party of Czechoslovakia, the international workers' and communist movement, and above all the findings of Soviet social science.
>
> Graduates in this field must display an awareness of social, political and moral responsibility, an awareness that they must answer for their work to the Communist Party and to the socialist social order. They must be able to stand actively, competently and firmly in ideological matters against all forms of anticommunism, revisionism and opportunism, and against all varieties of bourgeois ideology. (Vaněk 1980, p. 251; italics removed)

Another important sociological institution to be deeply affected by the process of Normalization after 1969 was the Czechoslovak Sociological Association. The overall assessment for the years 1969–1989 is mixed rather than entirely negative. The repressions of the early 1970s gave way to the slow and cautious development of genuinely professional activities which, in turn, evolved into more autonomous forms of sociological work in the later part of the 1980s (Petrusek 2002, pp. 186–187). The basic method of 'consolidation'—the systematic replacement of staff starting at the very top of the hierarchy and proceeding to successively lower levels, which was used by the pro-Soviet leaders to such overwhelming effect for regaining control over the Communist Party and academic institutions—was applied within the association as well. After the reform-oriented members of the governing bodies were replaced by party conformists in early 1970, the 'revitalized' main committee proceeded to dismiss all heads of sections and regional branches and to stage a 're-registration' of all members based on political loyalty and (flexibly defined) professional and scholarly qualifications. The number of members dropped from 1044 in 1969 to 526 in 1970 (Kahuda and Vacek 1973, pp. 313–319; Ulč 1978, p. 434, endn. 2).

The association lost any degree of autonomy it may have briefly enjoyed in the late 1960s, but it continued as the only professional platform for Czech sociologists. The renewal and expansion of the association's activities were a steady process, one documented by the reports from its general assemblies held every 3 years. Membership grew to 700 in 1980 and 919 in 1988. In 1976, the association began publishing a yearly newsletter. Its 12 sections and six regional branches held around 20 lectures, seminars and conferences, and published some four conference volumes every year. The section for methodology, usually the most active within the association, organized courses and seminars on general methodology, the philosophy of science, research techniques and, with increasing frequency during the 1980s, the use of computers and statistical software for data analysis. Ironically but not surprisingly, the section for Marxist sociological theory was more frequently reprimanded than any other for insufficient activity, which reflected many sociologists' tendency to avoid topics associated with the dominant ideology, as well as the isolation of the disciplinary elite, which was officially entrusted with developing theory, from the membership base. The section for methodology was also the largest, with 356 members in 1988. It was followed by the sections for the sociology of work and industry (309) and for the sociology of youth (282). These figures correspond with the most frequent affiliations of the association's members: one third were based at applied research institutes under various government ministries (34%), another third in industry, 20% at universities, and the rest at the Academy of Sciences or in various party and government bodies.

The data for the 1980s show two separate but equally noteworthy trends: the incipient feminization of the membership and its aging. The share of women members in the association grew from 34% in 1982 to 41% in 1988, while the share of female officials in the governing bodies remained constant at 25%. Over the same period, the proportion of members older than 40 rose from 58 to 68%, a trend that indicates that the cohort which had entered the discipline in the early 1970s was not succeeded by a similarly strong generation of younger sociologists.

Conclusion

Czech sociology during Normalization was in a dire shape, but it managed to survive and accumulate, within the limits of the possible, the knowledge and skills needed for the better times to come. The situation was complex, even paradoxical. On the one hand, the communist regime, driven as it was by the ideological assumption that socialist societies were the first in human history to be organized on truly scientific principles, was committed to maintaining an extensive research sector within the vast system of institutions that made up the structure of a centrally planned economy and society. On the other hand, the party's arbitrary power and its exercise of rigid ideological surveillance made any form of critical social science impossible. Normalization's academic—and worse still, human—cost to sociology was huge. It included truncated and terminated careers, the suboptimal allocation of talent to positions, widespread intellectual mediocrity, and provincialism. The discipline was damaged by an all-pervasive political opportunism in the choice and treatment of topics, its isolation from Western discussions, and the lack of continuity with the national sociological tradition of the pre-communist period (Voříšek 2014; Dianiška 1989). But at the same time, the discipline was allowed to reproduce itself. It could preserve most of the institutional achievements of the 1960s, provide training to the new generations, and even digest some of the theoretical and, above all, methodological advances in the West that managed to get through the Iron Curtain. Many Czech sociologists' commitment to the renewal of the discipline became increasingly visible as the regime began to lose control over society in the second half of the 1980s.

The signs of the system's weakness became unmistakable after Mikhail Gorbachev's ascent to power in the Soviet Union in 1985. The Czechoslovak hardliners who had been installed in power almost literally at Soviet gunpoint after 1968 could no longer rely on backing from Moscow, and worse than that, Soviet perestroika introduced a new discourse of openness which soon came to challenge the neo-Stalinist principles of the Czechoslovak regime. The slow beginnings of a more liberal climate made their way into official sociology in the form of new figures and new themes that were now allowed to appear in official institutions and publications. The changes were rather minimal at universities, which remained in a petrified state until the last days of communist rule (in Brno less so than in Prague), but liberalization was increasingly noticeable in the Academy of Sciences and in the sphere of applied research. Several new appointments were made to the editorial board of *Sociologický časopis*, and the journal started to publish pieces by, among others, the reformist Soviet sociologist Tatyana Zaslavskaya.

Nothing demonstrated the sea change that was about to take place better than the revolt of rank-and-file members against the party-appointed leadership at the 1988 general assembly of the Czechoslovak Sociological Association. In an unprecedented move, the election of the association's new governing body resulted in the removal of several pre-approved candidates, who saw themselves replaced by somewhat younger members with a superior professional reputation (Petrusek 2002,

p. 186). This was one event marking the ascent of a group of new disciplinary leaders (most of them born in the 1930s or 1940s), who had long ago abandoned any sympathy they might have had for Marxist–Leninist ideology and were full of enthusiasm for Western sociology with its, as they believed (based on little direct contact), significantly higher academic, and professional standards. This group came to dominate sociology in the Czech Republic after the political transition of 1989.

Notes

1. The most notable sociologists to emigrate in or after 1968 were: Bedřich Bauman (University of Canterbury, Christchurch, New Zealand, and Laurentian University, Ontario), Václav Lamser (University of Bielefeld), Zdeněk Strmiska (CNRS, Paris), Ivan Sviták (California State University, Chico), Ilja Šrubař (Universities of Konstanz and Erlangen-Nürnberg). It is worth observing that the Czech sociological emigration did not produce any international star sociologists comparable to exiles from other Central European countries such as Zygmunt Bauman or Iván Szelényi.
2. The 'Department for complex forecast modeling' specialized in the forecasting of sports activities in Czechoslovakia. Its head, Miloš Zeman, an economic forecaster, went on to become the Prime Minister and President of the Czech Republic after 1989. Václav Klaus, another economist and post-1989 Prime Minister and President, was among the contributors to the controversial volume.
3. A department of applied sociology was established at the university in Olomouc in 1971, but, interestingly, it did not offer any study program in sociology.

References

Alan, Josef [pseud. Čep, Lubor and Benedikt, Jan]. 1988. O sociologické obci. Sociologická skica (On sociological community: A sociological sketch). *Sociologický obzor* 2 (3): 6–12.

Allen, Michael Patrick. 1990. The 'quality' of journals in sociology reconsidered: Objective measurers of journal influence. *ASA Footnotes* 18 (9): 4–5.

Aragon, Louis. 1968. Ce roman que je tiens pour une oeuvre majeure. In Milan Kundera, *La plaisanterie,* i–vi. Paris: Gallimard.

Bucholc, Marta. 2016. *Sociology in Poland.* Basingstoke: Palgrave Macmillan.

Dianiška, Ivan. 1989. 'Konsolidovaná sociológia'—malá, ale naša! ('Consolidated sociology'—Small, but ours!). Paper given at the second congress of the Slovak Sociological Association, Martin, September 26–29.

Duffková, Jana. 1985. Poznámky k analýze významu a tematického zaměření diplomových prací studentů na katedře marxisticko-leninské sociologie filosofické fakulty Univerzity Karlovy (Notes on the analysis of meaning and thematic focus of diploma theses at the Department of Marxist–Leninist sociology at Faculty of Arts, Charles University). *Sociologický časopis* 21 (4): 425–429.

Fleck, Christian, and Andreas Hess. 2011. Sociology and communism: Coming to terms with a discipline's past. *Comparative Sociology* 10 (5): 670–690.

Fojtík, Jan. 1972. Situace na společenskovědním úseku a úkoly společenských věd po XIV. sjezdu KSČ (The situation in the field of social sciences and the tasks of social sciences after 14th party congress). *Nová mysl* 26 (2): 147–169.

Havel, Václav. 1992. Dear Dr. Husák. In *Open letters*, 50–83. New York: Vintage.

Hrzal, Ladislav. 1973. *Kritika soudobých sociologických a sociálně filosofických teorií* (A critique of contemporary sociological and social-philosophical theories). Prague: Svoboda.

Jareš, Jakub, Matěj Spurný, and Katka Volná (eds.). 2012. *Náměstí Krasnoarmějců 2: učitelé a studenti Filozofické fakulty UK v období normalizace* (Red Army Square 2: Teachers and students of the Faculty of Arts in the normalization period). Prague: Faculty of Arts, Charles University.

Kabele, Jiří. 2011. Sportpropag - nepravděpodobné místo pro studium společnosti: Osobní pohled (Sportpropag—An unlikely place for the study of society: A personal view). *Sociální studia* 8 (1): 17–35.

Kahuda, František, and Lubomír Vacek. 1973. Zpráva o valném shromáždění Československé sociologické společnosti (A report from the general assembly of the Czechoslovak Sociological Association). *Sociologický časopis* 9 (3): 313–323.

Konopásek, Zdeněk (ed.). 2000. *Our lives as database: Doing a sociology of ourselves: Czech social transitions in autobiographical research dialogues.* Prague: Karolinum.

Laiferová, Eva. 2014. Slovenská sociológia v klietke normalizácie (Slovak sociology in the cage of normalization). In *Sociológia v ére normalizácie—trinásť reflexií* (Sociology in the period of normalization—13 reflections), ed. Eva Laiferová and Ľudmila Mistríková, 13–42. Bratislava: Comenius University.

Machonin, Pavel et al. 1969. *Československá společnost* (Czechoslovak society). Bratislava: Epocha.

McDermott, Kevin. 2015. *Communist Czechoslovakia, 1945–89. A political and social history.* Basingstoke: Palgrave Macmillan.

Možný, Ivo. 2004. Brněnská anomálie? Brněnská sociologie 1963 až 1989 - subjektivní historie (The Brno anomaly? Sociology in Brno 1963–1989, a subjective history). *Sociologický časopis/Czech Sociological Review* 40 (5): 609–622.

Musil, Jiří. 2004. Poznámky o české sociologii za komunistického režimu (Remarks on Czech sociology under the communist regime). *Sociologický časopis/Czech Sociological Review* 40 (5): 573–595.

Nešpor, Zdeněk R. 2014. 'Šedá zóna' v éře tzv. normalizace: Dům techniky ČSVTS Pardubice v dějinách české sociologie (The 'grey zone' in the so-called Normalization period: The House of technology in Pardubice in the history of Czech sociology). *Sociologický časopis/Czech Sociological Review* 50 (1): 107–130.

Oates-Indruchová, Libora. 2008. The limits of thought? The regulatory framework of social sciences and humanities in Czechoslovakia (1968–1989). *Europe-Asia Studies* 60 (10): 1767–1782.

Petráň, Josef. 1998. Filosofická fakulta (The faculty of arts). In *Dějiny Univerzity Karlovy IV: 1918–1990*, ed. Jan Havránek and Zdeněk Pousta, 431–471. Prague: Karolinum.

Petrusek, Miloslav [pseud. Piluša, Martin]. 1988. *Sociologický časopis* ve světle kvantitativních dat (*Sociologický časopis* in the light of quantitative data). *Sociologický obzor* 2 (3): 27–36.

Petrusek, Miloslav. 2002. Peripetie Masarykovy české sociologické společnosti (nejen v letech 1989–2002) [The peripeties of the Masaryk Czech Sociological Association (not only in the years 1989–2002)]. *Sociologický časopis/Czech Sociological Review* 38 (1–2): 184–189.

Petrusek, Miloslav. 2004. Výuka sociologie v čase tání a v časech normalizace (1964–1989) [Teaching sociology in the periods of thaw and Normalization (1964–1989)]. *Sociologický časopis/Czech Sociological Review* 40 (5): 597–607.

Potůček, Martin (ed.). 1995. *Normalizace ve společenských vědách, můj život v normalizaci* (Normalization in the social sciences, my life in normalization). Prague: Institute of Sociological Studies, Charles University.

Prokůpek, Ladislav. 2002. Normalizace v Ústavu pro filosofii a sociologii ČSAV (Normalization in the Institute for Philosophy and Sociology of the Czechoslovak Academy of Sciences). In *Věda v Československu v období normalizace (1970–1975)*, ed. Antonín Kostlán, 201–217. Prague: Center for Research on History of Science.

Richta, Radovan. 1973. O stranický přístup k vědecké práci (For a party approach to scientific work). *Sociologický časopis* 9 (4): 337–339.

Sica, Alan, and Stephen Turner (eds.). 2005. *The disobedient generation: Social theorists in the sixties*. Chicago: University of Chicago Press.

Šiklová, Jiřina [pseud. Otava, Jiří]. 1988. Public opinion research in Czechoslovakia. *Social Research* 55 (1–2): 247–260.

Šiklová, Jiřina. 1990. The 'gray zone' and the future of dissent in Czechoslovakia. *Social Research* 57 (2): 347–363.

Šimečka, Milan. 1984. *The restoration of order: The normalization of Czechoslovakia, 1969–1976*. London: Verso.

Skovajsa, Marek (ed.). 2004. Česká sociologie v letech 1965–1989 (Czech sociology in 1965–1989. A roundtable discussion). *Sociologický časopis/Czech Sociological Review* 40 (5): 695–740.

Szelényi, Iván. 2012. Jiří Musil and the East European origins of the new urban sociology. *Sociologický časopis/Czech Sociological Review* 48 (6): 1156–1163.

Ulč, Otto. 1978. Some aspects of Czechoslovak society since 1968. *Social Forces* 57 (2): 419–435.

Urbánek, Eduard. 1994. Ups and downs in Czech sociology. In *Eastern Europe in transformation: The impact on sociology*, ed. Mike Forrest Keen and Janusz Mucha, 79–88. Westport, CT: Greenwood Press.

Vaněk, Antonín. 1980. Systém přípravy sociologů v ČSSR (The system of sociological training in the Czechoslovak Socialist Republic). *Sociologický časopis* 16 (5): 551–553.

Večerník, Jiří. 2011. Empirický výzkum chudoby v českých zemích ve třech historických obdobích (Empirical research on poverty in the Czech lands in three historical periods). *Data a výzkum - SDA Info* 5 (2): 133–146.

Voříšek, Michael. 2014. Česká sociologie sedmdesátých a osmdesátých let (Czech sociology of the 1970s and 1980s). In *Dějiny české sociologie* (The history of Czech sociology), ed. Zdeněk R. Nešpor, 358–384. Prague: Academia.

Wolchik, Sharon L. 2013. Doing political science research in Husák's Czechoslovakia. *Problems of Post-Communism* 60 (4): 22–27.

CHAPTER 6

The 1990s: Reconstruction and the Turn to the West

Abstract After the regime change in 1989, it seemed that Czech society had become an internationally relevant 'social laboratory' and sociologists would attain public recognition as producers of expert knowledge indispensable for the successful outcome of the transformation process. In the end, this role went to economics instead, and sociology was faced with a crisis of identity. This chapter describes how sociology in the Czech Republic was reconstructed in the 1990s, transforming from a small, politically controlled community into a solidly institutionalized discipline. It explores the ambivalences that accompanied the discipline's turn to the West and the formation of its new agenda, with special attention to its central interests.

Keywords Institutionalization · Post-communist transformation International collaboration · Intellectual agenda · Westernization

One of the most widespread metaphors employed in the rhetoric of revolutionary euphoria in 1989 referred to the nation's 'reawakening' after the long years of ideological oppression. Communism had collapsed and was almost universally believed to represent a discontinuity in the nation's history—something externally imposed that needed to be fought off. In his first New Year's address to the nation in 1990, President Václav Havel, a former dissident and 'enemy of the people,' spoke of the country's 'moral contamination' and considered an

M. Skovajsa and J. Balon, *Sociology in the Czech Republic*, Sociology Transformed, DOI 10.1057/978-1-137-45027-2_6

alternative way of organizing the political field—what he called 'nonpolitical politics' (Havel 1991, p. 391). Initially, the new visions of society's development were not conceived of simply as a transition from communism to capitalism. Soon, however, the intellectuals who had played a prominent role in the nonparty platform known as the Civic Forum that had landed a decisive win (53%) in the first free elections in June 1990 lost to technocrats led by Václav Klaus, the neoliberal economist who became the Czech Prime Minister in 1992. Since then, the 'transformation' of Czech society has been associated primarily with economic matters, while social and moral concerns have typically assumed only a secondary importance. To use the aforementioned metaphor, Czech society was to be 'reawakened' as a Western-oriented and economically developed country.

The expectations regarding the future of sociology were high. Czech society had become a 'social laboratory' that attracted the attention of Western researchers, a fact that facilitated the resumption of international contacts, which had been undercut during the communist era. Sociologists were also hopeful that their discipline would once again become politically relevant and publicly recognized. These hopes remained mostly unfulfilled, but on balance, the 1990s—'a decade of reconstruction' for sociology in Central and Eastern Europe (Keen and Mucha 2004)—can be evaluated positively. The disciplinary elite changed radically, but sociology's existing institutional base was preserved and even expanded. The way the field opened up to the 'world' (meaning mostly the West) was unprecedented, although in hindsight it was a somewhat one-sided endeavor. The discipline's successful reboot also involved a major reorganization and updating of its intellectual agenda.

A Reconstructed Institutional Setting

Looking at the basic institutional arrangements from which sociology in the Czech Republic began its struggle for resurgence in the post-1989 period, one may be surprised by the apparent continuity of the discipline's development. Although its setting had long remained the same, sometimes, to put it in Weberian terms, 'there comes a moment when the atmosphere changes' (Weber 1949, p. 111). In November 1989, the façade of the old regime was torn down, and it soon became clear that the change would not be just short-lived. Numerous alternative visions appeared almost immediately after the November events, most notably a plan for sociology's renewal as formulated by a group of Czech sociologists who would soon become the new intellectual and institutional leaders of the discipline, namely Jiří Musil, Miloslav Petrusek, Martin Potůček, and Josef Alan. These visions were put forward in a coordinated manner by the Sociological Forum, which was established as early as December 7, 1989 as an alternative to the official Czechoslovak Sociological Association. Their first proposals characteristically addressed the 'return of excluded figures into academic and scientific structures, the radical transformation of the organizational structure of sociological instruction and, naturally, the annulment of the officially accredited "Marxist-Leninist sociology" as a field of study' (Petrusek 2002, p. 186).

In a matter of only several months, the whole environment changed beyond recognition. Personnel replacement rejuvenated sociology regardless of the fact that many of those who returned to the academic sphere would, in another country, have been close to emeritus age. At the institutional level, the clash between previously marginalized academics and the discipline's old officials played out more smoothly at the higher echelons of the hierarchy. Those persons associated with the old regime could hardly expect to be considered representative of the new direction. As a result, in the first months after November 1989 almost all top academic positions were filled with new people, both at the Czechoslovak Academy of Sciences and at major universities. In January 1990, only four out of 78 high-ranking representatives of Charles University in Prague (the rector and deputy rectors, deans, and deputy deans) had held their positions before November 1989 (Havránek and Pousta 1998, pp. 584–586).

These changes proved to be much more complicated at the lower levels of academic life, especially at the level of university departments where the number of positions had been very low. The re-entry of sociologists who had worked outside academic structures before 1989—in many cases for almost two decades—was met with resistance. One of them, Jiřina Šiklová, described this reluctance thus:

> Will we go back to our professions? When no one wants us there? One employee who was given the job of dealing with the cases of the people dismissed for political reasons complained: 'Those people from '68 still want the top jobs. They were in the leading posts in 1968: when they left the faculty they were leading figures in the opposition, and now we're

supposed to take them back into leading posts again.' And it was not intended as a joke. (Šiklová 1990, p. 361)

This lack of flexibility, combined with the imminent expansion of the higher education system, prompted efforts aimed at creating new academic niches and resulted in a series of developments on the institutional level. In 1990, another returnee, Miloslav Petrusek, co-founded the Faculty of Social Sciences at Charles University in Prague, thus placing a new department of sociology on the institutional map in addition to the existing sociology departments at the Faculty of Arts at Charles University and at Masaryk University in Brno. Also that year, a department of sociology and adult education was established at Palacký University in Olomouc. This extraordinary foundational momentum soon slowed down, but the social science departments at the university in Brno expanded rapidly over the 1990s, eventually resulting in the creation of a new Faculty of Social Studies in 1998.

These institutional changes laid the foundations for the open environment that prevailed in the social sciences for the years to come. The creation of new academic posts facilitated the process of transitional justice for the victims of political persecution during the communist period. The new institutional settings were also instrumental in satisfying calls for more differentiated forms of instruction, interdisciplinary programs and unrestricted notions of what the discipline's agenda should be. In terms of student numbers, Czech sociology departments continued to grow steadily in the first decade after 1989, although they remained small when compared with the explosion after 2000 (see Chap. 7), with at most a few dozen new students a year until 1995. The department of sociology in Brno started with 12–15 new entrants in the early 1990s, a number similar to the situation in the 1980s. In 1995 the figure increased to 35, and from 1998 to the early 2000s it fluctuated between 70 and 75 a year. Similar trends in student enrollment could be seen at the department of sociology at the Faculty of Social Sciences in Prague, where sociology was taught in a joint BA program along with public and social policy. When the number 'jumped' to 45 in 1995, several members of the department publicly expressed serious concerns about the future of the discipline suggesting that the retreat of direct student–teacher interaction would undermine sociology's main strengths (Šanderová 1995).

There was, of course, one question which was of crucial importance for sociology's recovery as a research-oriented discipline at the time. This was the resumption of an independent Institute of Sociology at the Academy of Sciences. The process of sociology striking out on its own—after being part of a joint Institute of Philosophy and Sociology for almost two decades—was a rather precarious one, as it took place in the unclear situation of the Academy's own chaotic transformation.[1] The urban sociologist Jiří Musil, the first director of the 'new' Institute, recalls that the Academy was

> an extremely complicated social structure, in which—though only for a short moment—ideological protagonists of 'real socialism', [former] secret police agents, people with ties to the dissident circle, persons coming from the sociological periphery, sociologists who had returned to their profession, and also persons who did not really know what sociology actually is about had to work together. (Musil 2006, p. 190)

After initial plans for renewing the Institute as an interdisciplinary research center that would combine rigorous sociological methods with theoretical, historical, and cultural approaches were abandoned, it was split up into eight more conventional departments. Its research activities were focused mainly on various aspects of the 'transformation,' and gradually reached a distinctive profile especially in the departments of economic sociology, gender and sociology, local and regional development, political sociology, social stratification, and social structure and modernization. Although at one point the number of researchers dropped to 50 because of massive cuts at the Academy, the Institute survived and continued to play a key role in developing a culture of research at a time when sociology seemed capable only of scratching out a living either as a teaching enterprise or as a distinguished name for commercialized public opinion polls and applied market research.

The intense involvement of the discipline's leading figures in institution-building also had its downside. In 1990, the Czech part of what was then the Czechoslovak Sociological Association was renamed the Masaryk Czech Sociological Association, and after the break-up of Czechoslovakia in 1993 it became an independent national association. Its founders expected it to act as an open and unrestricted platform for collaborative activities, picking up where the intellectual outburst from the 1968 period had left off. At first, the number of members hovered around 900. After the initial enthusiasm had subsided, this number dropped to some 300 members and has remained more or less the same ever since (Petrusek 2003, p. 57). Although the association organized several notable meetings, such as the 1995 conference on the transformation of Czech society, its role in the professional life of sociologists in the Czech Republic was marginal [no new sections were formed until after 2005, when the range of activities began to expand again (Šubrt 2012)]. To be fair, overcommitted institution-builders were not the only reason why the national association spent more than a decade after 1989 in the doldrums.[2] The abrupt regime change and the hardships of transformation also led to the absence of an active middle-aged generation during this period.

Whereas the (re)establishment of national institutions produced notably lasting results, the only example of a transnational institution-building project, the Prague campus of the Central European University (CEU), founded in 1991 by the billionaire philanthropist George Soros, resulted in failure and closure in 1996.[3] This university's department of sociology began regular instruction in autumn 1991, when it opened a 1-year postgraduate program entitled 'Society and Politics.' Annual enrollment remained roughly the same during the school's entire Prague period (about 40, peaking at 45 in 1994/1995), with applications increasing significantly from 125 in 1991 to 239 in 1994 (Pospíšilová 2013, p. 72). The number of new students entering the sociology program at CEU exceeded those at any other Czech sociology department. Although the idea of CEU as an independent Western-type institution was initially welcomed by Czech political and academic representatives, it gradually began to be seen as an entity that was alien to the local academic environment and its historically embedded patterns of regulation and control. A series of circumstances—CEU's unfulfilled expectation to receive a permanent building from the Czech government, a sudden two-thirds reduction in the state's approved contribution in 1993, the fact that for its entire Prague period the university could operate only as a foundation with programs accredited either in the USA or Great Britain and that it never attained official university status inside the country—led to CEU's permanent withdrawal from Prague in 1996, after having transferred its sociology program to Warsaw a year before. Various observers have interpreted the history of this endeavor as showing Czech political and academic elites' unwillingness to open the national higher education system to alternatives rooted in an international academic environment (Čerych 1995; Bryant 2000; Pospíšilová 2013). Regardless of all possible explanations (personal and political animosity against Soros, resentment toward Western models, or the cluelessness of regulatory institutions), the fact remains that in the mid-1990s the Czech academic landscape lost a Western-type university institution that might have helped to disrupt the homogeneity of local academic life and made the channels of international mobility available to Czech sociologists as well.

Restocking with Western Products

The starting point of Czech sociology's renewal after 1989, to recall Thomas Kuhn's account of the revolutionary phases in the history of science (Kuhn 1962), might be best described as reflecting a situation when 'the old' is doomed to be displaced and 'the new' has not yet been thoroughly installed. In addition, the turn to the West and attempts to re-establish continuity with international developments in the discipline, were taking place at a time when world sociology was rife with serious doubts about its mission and prospects. It was not entirely impossible that the first text an aspiring Czech sociologist eager to learn about sociological theory undistorted by Marxism–Leninism might choose to read would be Steven Seidman's 'The end of sociological theory,' which claimed that Western sociological theory was in fact 'a totalizing theory of society' and had 'lost most of its social and intellectual importance' (Seidman 1991, p. 131). Nor did it help to read what the field's other authorities were saying at the time, for instance, Peter Rossi claimed in 1990 that it was pretty obvious that 'something is wrong with sociology' (Rossi 1990, p. 623). Modernization theory, which was an obvious reference point for Czech sociologists interested in the logic of the social change that was taking place then and there, had long ago lost its universal appeal and was thus unable to provide a generally acceptable vocabulary that they would be eager to use.

This notwithstanding, the 1990s were marked by the reception of Western discourses and the 'restocking' of the sociological corpus of knowledge with both intellectual and material goods of Western provenience. Indeed, this is true even in the literal, material sense. Although it would be an exaggeration to claim that Czech libraries were completely empty, the shortage of relevant literature was a ubiquitous obstacle for the learning and teaching of sociology. This shortage was an unavoidable part of sociologists' lives in the Czech Republic in the 1990s, irrespective of whether they were junior or senior academics, and helped to reproduce a sense of missed opportunities. Miloslav Petrusek, a leading institution-builder and agenda-setter at the same time, aptly expressed these feelings when he reflected on a visit made to the library at the University of Konstanz, Germany, in 1995 after 'long years of traveling abstinence':

> I have found myself in the library of Babel where you could find anything, everything from Parsons and everything against Parsons, all references to Parsons and everything the great Parsons himself plagiarized. There was all of Weber on about seven huge shelves with commentaries one cannot peruse in a lifetime, there were Marxists and anti-communists, there were renowned and obscure authors, and also authors unknown to anybody for a long time and who would probably never be approached by anybody again – but who knows? At first I was desperate, but then I decided to be a Babelian librarian and bring things into order. I started to study the concepts of which I had almost no notion as a result of that twenty-year-long intellectual chasm – meaning interpretative sociology, phenomenology, ethnomethodology – and I did not understand anything. But there were catalogues to catalogues, dictionaries to dictionaries, the sun was shining … (Petrusek 2006, pp. 11–12)

This urge to 'bring things into order' was particularly characteristic of the first years after 1989, which were the heyday of all sorts of compendia and handbooks summarizing the theory, methodology, and history of the entire discipline or its various subfields. The most important project of this kind was the 1600-page *Great dictionary of sociology* which grew out of a collective effort initiated still before 1989 (Maříková et al. 1996). The downside of this primarily didactic tendency was the widespread notion that once sociology in the Czech Republic had become free to absorb Western influences, it should not try to do much more than that.

This aspect of the discipline's state in the 1990s can be illustrated with an excursion into the field of sociological theory. Given the persisting effects of the discipline's long international isolation before 1989, combined with the fact that most Czech sociologists preferred to read books in Czech, translations, and introductory textbooks were an especially important part of the process of restocking. The question of which Western sociologists representing certain ways of doing theory were translated or otherwise presented to the local readership thus became of crucial importance. In the 1990s, the writings of Zygmunt Bauman, revered at the time as the high priest of postmodern sociology, were formative for the newly emerging canon of sociological theory in the Czech Republic, as were articles and books disseminating the basic theories of, among others, Anthony Giddens, Pierre Bourdieu, and Ulrich Beck. The only local competitor to emerge at the time was the Czech strand of postmodern thinking epitomized by the writings of Václav Bělohradský, an émigré sociologist based in Italy and an influential public intellectual. Through his work, students were exposed to a sociology that favored an essayistic approach in the form of associative streams of thought on current matters of social and political life (e.g., Bělohradský 2011). Sociological theory either resigned itself to a certain type of commentary on the latest events or became identified with expository literature on the work of prestigious Western authors who could not be adequately studied in the preceding period. This pastiche-like practice of filling in the gaps is one of the most ingrained legacies of the 1990s. The 'restocking' of theoretical knowledge thus typically took on the form of compilations and only rarely inspired genuine original work.

As exceptions to this situation, we can cite two original contributions based on well-developed theoretical arguments (both have characteristically never been translated into English). Ivo Možný's short book *Why so easily?* Provided a sociological account of the so-called Velvet Revolution (Možný 1991). Using Bourdieu's theoretical framework, Možný argued that the collapse of communism had resulted from the changing relationship between the family and the Communist Party, accompanied by the corresponding conversions between various forms of capital. The other example is Jiří Kabele's study of post-communist transformation in terms of narrative and constructive processes. His book *Regeneration: principles of social construction* (Kabele 1998, cf. 2010) was one of a few which deployed Western conceptual resources for an original solution to general theoretical problems, especially the agency/structure dilemma.

The Formation of a Disciplinary Agenda

Apart from the unifying issue of transformation, which will be dealt with later in this chapter, any attempt at summarizing the shared interests of sociologists in the Czech Republic during the 1990s is bound to run into difficulty. There was one obvious difference compared to the situation before 1989: the state no longer had any direct political or ideological influence on the formation of the disciplinary agenda. Early in the decade, Czech sociologists were left alone in their effort to form a disciplinary identity—it was not until the late 1990s that the state began to systematically define its priorities, mainly by providing funding for issues related to the European Union accession process.

With the removal of political control after 1989, but with limited international experience and limited knowledge of foreign languages (along with a sudden devaluation of the command of Russian), national publication outlets experienced something of a boom. The 'flagship' (but no longer the only) national journal *Sociologický časopis* was poised to take a central position in Czech sociologists' publication strategies due to the fact that it was the country's only sociology journal with an 'impact factor.' In 1990, it underwent an instant change in identity from being the official journal of Marxist-Leninist sociology into a review that aspired for international relevance. For the next 10 years, it was the central platform for studying the post-communist transformation and the newly emerging political system, but also new disciplinary subfields and niches such as gender, civil society, and globalization. Since 1992, when its English-language edition was launched, the journal has also served as a vehicle for communicating with the international community (with the unintended consequence of channeling the energies of many Czech authors away from publishing in Western journals). Other journals were quick to emerge, but some did not survive the early era of enthusiasm. This was the case with the *Sociologické aktuality* (*Sociological Newsletter*, 1989–1994) and *S-Obzor* (*S-Horizon,* 1992–1995), the successor to a samizdat journal aimed at promoting a new paradigm of critical sociology (Havelka 1993, p. 529). More successful in challenging the dominance of the Prague-based and quantitatively oriented *Sociologický časopis* were other two journals founded in the course of the 1990s: the review for qualitative and biographical sociology *Biograf* and the generalist journal *Sociální studia* (*Social Studies*) published by the Brno faculty.

Developments in the book publishing sector were less straightforward, due to the collapse of the communist-era publishing industry and its chaotic privatization soon after 1989, but sociology would go on to benefit from the gradual increase in the number of both public and private publishers that followed. The most important among these has been SLON (Sociological Publishing House), founded in 1991, which is the only Czech publisher to exclusively focus on sociological and related literature (see Červinková 2012, p. 1172). In the 1991–2000 period, SLON released 79 books (21 by foreign authors). Since many of its titles were textbooks, introductory texts to various disciplinary areas and translations, SLON was instrumental in making reliable teaching materials available to the rapidly growing body of students. Somewhat later, sociological books began to be published by the two most prestigious academic publishing houses of the post-1989 period, Academia (under the Academy of Sciences) and Karolinum (Charles University Press). By the year 2000, a group of small private publishers had emerged that were eager to make moderate, but still some, profits on books that did not sell but that were subsidized from public research funds. At the same time, many books, edited volumes, and working papers continued to be published by academic institutions themselves, a common practice inherited from before 1989 that often went hand in hand with weak and only formal peer review.

The massive political change and the correspondingly radical shift in discourse put many academics trained in Marxist-Leninist scholarship, who had been thoroughly isolated from Western literature, in the position of beginners. Judged by the standards of Western academic culture, many of the publications produced in this period can be barely considered to represent original research work. For instance, a fairly large number of articles on sociological theory published in *Sociologický časopis* can at best be described as good introductions to some theoretical issue, or at worst as excerpts from a Western book, written with a questionable approach to referencing. Many of the texts produced at the time took the form of internal reports, mimeographed research papers, anthologies, conference proceedings, unpublished textbook chapters, and reviews. In the transition period, being an academic did not entail an imperative to publish, and publication output defined academic merit only to a limited extent. Given the persistence of the pre-1989 division of academic labor—with research concentrated at the Academy while the universities primarily engaged in educational activities, though now with the added burden of having to cope with the reform of higher education—it is no surprise that the observable publication patterns tend to mirror the research interests of particular departments or centers within the Academy's Institute of Sociology more than anything else.

The dominant themes of sociological publications in the 1990s were the post-communist transformation in general, the dynamics of social structure and stratification, socio-economic changes and the social aspects of economic transformation, social problems and social policy issues, and the new political and administrative system (Illner 2002, p. 203). The principal interests of sociology in the Czech Republic during the first decade after 1989 can be also gleaned from figures concerning the types of articles published in *Sociologický časopis*. The largest group fell under the rubric 'Governments and Political Power' (14.5% of all articles) and encompassed mainly texts on the new political system. Articles in the category 'Transformation' made up 12.3%, while 'Stratification and the Class Structure of Society' ranked third with 11%. The authors' institutional affiliations were as follows: 43% of the articles were authored by researchers from the Academy of Sciences, 30% from Charles University in Prague, and 15% from Masaryk University in Brno (Vohralíková 2002, p. 144). The dominance of these three disciplinary centers is also reflected in the allocation of research funding during this period. Researchers had limited access to public funding in the early 1990s (with the exception of those working at the Academy, where an in-house grant agency was founded in 1990). This changed with the formation of the Czech Science Foundation (GA ČR) in 1993, which soon established itself as the principal national grant-distributing agency for basic research. Its funding of sociology projects in the 1993–2000 period was almost exclusively to the benefit of the dominant centers: of 60 projects, 22 went to Charles University, 20 to the Academy of Sciences, and 17 to Masaryk University (Vohralíková 2002, p. 146).

While the institutional map remained more or less the same in the middle to late 1990s, there were visible shifts in disciplinary profiles and agendas. The various departments of sociology developed disparate research specializations, the most distinctive being 'biographic sociology' and 'applied research' at Prague's Faculty of Social Sciences, 'criminology' and 'sociology of work' at Prague's Faculty of Arts, and 'minorities,' 'sociology of the family,' and 'population studies' in Brno (see Illner 2002; Petrusek 2003; Nešpor 2014, pp. 525–529). Despite this differentiation and the related increase in competitive tensions, in the 1990s there was no return of anything like the deep antagonism between the Prague and Brno groups that had existed during the interwar period (see Chap. 3)—an unfortunate fact, if we consider that a clash of well-articulated views might have helped to stimulate debate regarding larger theoretical and methodological issues and the distinctive role and mission of sociology in the Czech Republic. If any intellectual controversies appeared at all, they were typically inter-departmental at the Academy or intra-departmental at the universities.

Due in large measure to the delayed reception of international influences during the communist era, sociology's intellectual landscape in the Czech Republic after 1989 was dominated by the notorious old tensions, which emerged with increased intensity, although they turned out to be rather short-lived. Disciplinary debates were structured around such binary oppositions as macro versus micro, or value-neutral versus critical sociology, but probably the most heated exchanges were related to the split between hermeneutic or biographic methods on the one hand and the quantitative positivist tradition on the other. Although nearly every defense of a thesis based on qualitative methods seemed to involve a spirited discussion of the scientific rigor of grounded theory or of what use could ever be the information distilled from just four interviews, eventually the conflict dissipated and qualitative approaches found their institutional niches, especially at the universities, thanks to their continued popularity among students.

The 1990s were also when gender studies arrived on the academic scene in the Czech Republic. In the culturally conservative and male-dominated academic environment, the field's institutionalization did not proceed without difficulties and gender studies were often downplayed as pure activism (see Šmejkalová 2004). Research and teaching were at first pursued mainly by two Prague-based institutions: the department of Gender & Sociology, founded in 1990 at the Academy of Sciences' Institute of Sociology and which started publishing the journal *Gender, rovné příležitosti, výzkum* (*Gender & Research*) in 2000; and the non-profit organization Gender Studies, established in 1991, that among other activities organized lectures on gender issues for Czech universities. It was not before the turn of the millennium that gender studies began to take root as a study program at the universities. The first specialized center was set up within the department of social work at Charles University's Faculty of Arts in 1998. Two years later, however, the Faculty declined to accept a seed grant from the Ford Foundation for developing a fully-fledged academic program in gender studies, and its Academic Senate, which is composed of fellow academics and students, dissolved the center on the grounds that gender studies were not one of this Faculty's priorities. The gender studies group moved to the same university's Faculty of Humanities, where a department was established and an MA study program opened in 2004 (Sokolová 2014, pp. 591–592). Simultaneously, a BA program in gender studies was started at Brno's Faculty of Social Studies.

Czech Sociologists and Their 'Transformation' in the International Context

In 1995, Petr Matějů, an internationally recognized sociologist of social stratification, launched a debate on the 'post-totalitarian trauma of Czech sociology' with a paper presented at a conference in Prague sponsored by the International Sociological Association (ISA). This paper, which was originally intended for an international audience, was published in *Sociologický časopis* along with rejoinders from other leading Czech sociologists. Matějů, himself a key protagonist of the Czech debate on 'transformation,' hoped to trigger a discussion on the state of Czech sociology by raising two suggestive questions: 'Why is the image of Czech sociology on the international scene so vague, especially when compared to the image that Hungarian and Polish sociology are forming about themselves?' and 'Is Czech sociology heading toward a better future as a result of the political and economic changes that have occurred in our society since the collapse of the totalitarian regime?' (Matějů 1995, p. 255). The questions were consistent with the fact that Czech sociology's mission at the time was primarily perceived to consist in supplying expert knowledge for successfully managing the process of social and economic transformation. For example, Eduard Urbánek had written in another context that the major task facing Czech sociology was to 'facilitate the implementation of the economic transformation' (Urbánek 1994, p. 87). However, the expectation that sociology in the Czech Republic would find its fulfillment in the service of economic reform was never fulfilled. Instead, the public debate on 'transformation' was soon dominated by economics. Sociology lost. Economists, who figured prominently among the political leaders of the day, took a pretty straightforward view of society emphasizing, in line with their neoliberal ideological outlook, the free market, privatization, and the minimal role of the state (see Eyal 2000, pp. 71–79).

In his paper, Matějů went on to argue that—unlike economics as both an academic discipline and a tool of the reform process (which Prime Minister Klaus first declared 'finished' as early as 1993)—sociology had been pushed to the periphery on the grounds that it was 'capable, at best, of producing only a few ideological schemes, which moreover still possessed a relatively strong "socialist flavor"' (Matějů 1995, p. 256). The follow-up debate to the article (which continued for an entire year) focused on two recurring issues: sociology's participation in the 'transformation' and its position on the academic scene. One discussant, Jiří Kabele, felt that it would take at least two generations before sociology would be able to say anything substantial about the 'transformation' as a whole, and thus a more urgent challenge facing the discipline in the Czech Republic was how to reconstitute itself academically (Kabele 1995, pp. 263–266). Others argued that sociology's absence from the public scene was simply due to the fact that, given the speed of the economist-driven reform process, the social consequences of the reform had not yet landed on the political agenda of the day (Potůček 1995; Machonin 1995). All in all, this debate on sociology's identity crisis disclosed that Czech sociologists, unlike Czech economists, lacked an overarching theoretical (and ideological) vision of 'transformation.'

Despite the fact that many participants in the debate on the 'post-totalitarian trauma' expressed reservations toward identifying sociology with the implementation of economic reforms, the issue of 'transformation' undoubtedly functioned as an integrative project that was part of the systemic agenda for sociology in the Czech Republic in the 1990s. The two most distinctive approaches were the one represented by Pavel Machonin and his team, which in 1991 initiated a large survey entitled *Transformation of social structure* (first planned as an updated version of the 1967 study on the stratification of Czechoslovak society, see Chap. 4), and the one personified by Petr Matějů and Jiří Večerník, whose *Social report on the Czech Republic, 1989–1998* (Večerník and Matějů 1999) made use of the data gathered by the large survey *Economic expectations and attitudes*, conducted annually from 1990 to 1998 (Krejčí and Čížek 2014, p. 566). These two teams worked from different and often opposite assumptions: Machonin's team represented the traditional approach grounded in the 1960s reform Marxist thought and modernization theory, while Matějů and Večerník's group shared many of the principles of the economic reforms, to which Machonin et al. were opposed (Petrusek 2003, pp. 58–59).

Although the teams produced numerous publications (e.g., Machonin and Tuček 1996; Večerník 1996; Matějů and Vlachová 1999), their aim was not to elaborate an overarching theory of the transformation process that could be applied within the study of large-scale social change in other parts of the world. With the exception of Pavel Machonin and Jaroslav Krejčí's book *Czechoslovakia, 1918–1992: a laboratory of social change*—in which the authors sought to 'explore the fundamental social changes from the birth of the Czechoslovak nation-state to its dissolution' (Machonin and Krejčí 1996, p. 3; see also Machonin 1997)—the work of Czech sociologists did not show much interest in more general problems of society's development. Quite often, discussions of the 'transformation' tended to serve as nothing more than a ritualized introduction to the analysis of the particular data. Given the ubiquity of this catchword at the time, even those authors who studied a fairly specific topic were expected to frame it in terms of the general issue of 'transformation.'

The Czech version of 'transformation studies' formed a specific discourse that was met with some international response, paralleled maybe by the response to the Czech discourse on civil society, although here Czech sociologists' contribution was certainly less visible (e.g., Marada 1996). International collaborative projects related to the 'transformation' and the more general cross-country longitudinal survey programs[4] helped to reinforce sociology's credibility and relevance within the broader academic community. Most importantly, 'transformation studies' helped to restore a sense of continuity in social science research. As a constant activity during the entire 1990s, it produced large sets of data, numerous social reports, and other materials that are open to further investigation (the Czech Social Science Data Archive was founded at the Academy's Institute of Sociology in 1998). All of this was a great step forward compared to the situation in the preceding decades, when official policy had been to keep any knowledge on the state of society a secret. In light of this, it may be surprising to note that to date no one has undertaken to write a summary appreciation of the 1990s literature on the 'transformation' in the Czech Republic.

Another striking aspect of Czech sociologists' contribution to international debates concerning social change in the first decade after 1989 is that they were almost completely absent from the emerging discourse on post-socialism and post-communism. Although Czech authors wrote a good number of books, articles, and conference papers featuring 'post-socialism,' 'post-communism,' and similar terms in their title, most of the time these words were merely symbols for the particular period and region—the texts themselves had little to say about the issues pursued within the study of post-socialism or post-communism. As a result of this failure to engage in the broader theoretical contexts, the work of Czech sociologists found little international resonance. Western authors limited their attention to formulaic accounts of the events of November 1989, references to Václav Havel and a summary treatment (across multiple countries) of the main transitional processes such as privatization, the restitution of private property, the rehabilitation of the victims of political persecution, or the vetting of former secret police collaborators. This is perhaps best illustrated by the fact that even the most ambitious Western works in this area, such as William Outhwaite and Larry Ray's *Social theory and postcommunism* (2005), can make no reference to any Czech book, article or author other than, rather significantly, Havel's essay on 'anti-political politics' and one of his speeches about the need for transcendence in the postmodern world.

Conclusion

In the formative decade after 1989, sociology in the Czech Republic became a differentiated—and often also fragmented—discipline that reconnected with its earlier achievements in some areas (such as social stratification research, urban and regional sociology, or the sociology of work and industrial sociology) and set out from more modest starting positions in others. Czech sociologists' engagement and sense of responsibility for their discipline in this period were remarkable. Their fundamental concern was probably best captured in the then-popular—and now discredited—concept of 'catching up' with the West. In the specific case of Czech sociology, which had been kept in isolation from crucial developments in world sociology for 20 years, this motivation stimulated a broad range of activities that met with varying degrees of success. Despite significant institutional and intellectual advances, it was no less the case that the Westernizing push went hand in hand with a growing dependence on external models. Calls to 'internationalize' the discipline resulted in a propensity to uncritically absorb Western trends and novelties.

Notes

1. The number of the Academy of Sciences' employees dropped by one-third in 1992 and after budget restrictions in 1993 it decreased by one half when compared to the state in 1989 (from 13,896 in 1989 to 7127

in 1993—social sciences and humanities decreased by 57%—from 2420 in 1989 to 1046 in 1993, headcount) (Provazník et al. 1998, p. 36).

2. Out of ten sections existing in the early 1990s only two were regularly active at the end of the decade (sociology of agriculture and social deviance) (Petrusek 2003, p. 57).
3. The idea of a 'Central European university' first emerged in 1989. Originally, it was institutionalized as an alliance of two organizations—CEU in Prague and CEU in Budapest (Pospíšilová 2013, p. 31). Jiří Musil became the director of CEU's Prague branch in 1992.
4. These two types of projects included: International Social Justice Project (ISJP), Social Stratification in Eastern Europe after 1989 (SSEE), Social Consequences of Transition (SOCO), International Social Survey Program (ISSP), or European Values Study (EVS) (Večerník 2014).

References

Bělohradský, Václav. 2011. The post-communist manifesto. *Human Affairs* 21 (1): 62–69.

Bryant, Christopher. 2000. *George Soros, the Central European University and sociology*. Salford: Institute for Social Research of the University of Salford.

Červinková, Hana. 2012. Miloslav (Milan) Petrusek (1936–2012). *Sociologický časopis/Czech Sociological Review* 48 (6): 1171–1174.

Čerych, Ladislav. 1995. Educational reform in Central and Eastern Europe. *European Journal of Education* 30 (4): 423–435.

Eyal, Gil. 2000. Anti-politics and the spirit of capitalism: Dissidents, monetarists, and the Czech transition to capitalism. *Theory and Society* 29 (1): 49–92.

Havel, Václav. 1991. *Open letters: Selected writings, 1965–1990*. New York: Vintage Books.

Havelka, Miloš. 1993. S-OBZOR – neformální sociologický časopis (S-Horizon – an informal sociological journal). *Sociologický časopis* 29 (4): 529–531.

Havránek, Jan, and Zdeněk Pousta (eds.). 1998. *Dějiny Univerzity Karlovy IV (1918–1990)* (The history of Charles University IV. (1918–1990)). Prague: Karolinum.

Illner, Michal. 2002. Sociology - Czech Republic. In *Three social science disciplines in Central and Eastern Europe: Handbook on economics, political science and sociology (1989–2001)*, ed. Max Kaase, Vera Sparschuh, and Agnieszka Wenninger, 405–424. Berlin/Bonn: Social Science Information Centre/Collegium Budapest.

Kabele, Jiří. 1995. Trauma sociologie a české čekání na druhý dech (The sociology's trauma and the Czech waiting for a second breath of life). *Sociologický časopis* 31 (2): 263–266.

Kabele, Jiří. 1998. *Přerody – principy sociálního konstruování* (Regeneration—principles of social construction). Prague: Karolinum.

Kabele, Jiří. 2010. The agency/structure dilemma: A coordination solution. *Journal for the Theory of Social Behaviour* 40 (3): 314–338.

Keen, Mike F., and Janusz Mucha. 2004. Sociology in Central and Eastern Europe in the 1990s: A decade of reconstruction. *European Societies* 6 (2): 123–147.

Krejčí, Jaroslav, and Pavel Machonin. 1996. *Czechoslovakia, 1918–1992: A laboratory for social change*. London: Palgrave Macmillan.

Krejčí, Jindřich, and Tomáš Čížek. 2014. Empirická sociologie (Empirical sociology). In *Dějiny české sociologie* (The history of Czech sociology), ed. Zdeněk R. Nešpor, 560–573. Prague: Academia.

Kuhn, Thomas. 1962. *The structure of scientific revolutions*. Chicago: Univesity of Chicago Press.

Machonin, Pavel. 1995. K důkladnější analýze příčin problémů české sociologie (Towards a more thorough analysis of the causes of Czech sociology's problems). *Sociologický časopis* 31 (3): 357–360.

Machonin, Pavel, and Milan Tuček (eds.). 1996. *Česká společnost v transformaci. K proměnám sociální struktury* (Czech society in transformation: On the changes of social structure). Prague: SLON.

Machonin, Pavel. 1997. *Social transformation and modernization: On building theory of societal changes in the post-communist European countries*. Prague: SLON.

Marada, Radim. 1996. Power, money, and the good: Civil society between the state and market. *Sociální studia/Social studies* 1 (1): 43–54.

Maříková, Hana, Miloslav Petrusek, and Alena Vodáková (eds.). (1996). *Velký sociologický slovník* (The great sociological dictionary). Prague: Karolinum.

Matějů, Petr. 1995. Posttotalitní trauma české sociologie (The post-totalitarian trauma of Czech sociology). *Sociologický časopis* 31 (2): 255–258.

Matějů, Petr, and Klára Vlachová (eds.). 1999. *Nerovnost, spravedlnost, politika. Česká Republika 1991–1998* (Inequality, justice, politics. Czech Republic 1991–1998). Prague: SLON.

Možný, Ivo. 1991. *Proč tak snadno ... Některé rodinné důvody sametové revoluce* (Why so easy ... Some family reasons of velvet revolution). Prague: SLON.

Musil, Jiří. 2006. Poznámky ke čtyřiceti letům Sociologického ústavu AV ČR (Notes to 40 years of existence of the Institute of Sociology AS CR). *Sociologický časopis/Czech Sociological Review* 42 (1): 189–191.

Nešpor, Zdeněk R. 2014. Organizační zázemí akademického života (The organizational base of academic life). In *Dějiny české sociologie* (The history of Czech sociology), ed. Zdeněk R. Nešpor, 524–537. Prague: Academia.

Outhwaite, William, and Larry Ray. 2005. *Social theory and postcommunism*. Oxford: Blackwell.

Petrusek, Miloslav. 2002. Peripetie Masarykovy české sociologické společnosti (nejen v letech 1989–2002) (The peripeties of the Masaryk Czech Sociological Association (not only in years 1989–2002)). *Sociologický časopis/ Czech Sociological Review* 38 (1–2): 184–189.

Petrusek, Miloslav. 2003. Sociology in the Czech Republic after 1989. In *Sociology in Central and Eastern Europe: Transformations at the dawn of a new millennium*, ed. Mike Keen and Janusz Mucha, 49–60. Westport, CT: Praeger Publishers.

Petrusek, Miloslav. 2006. *Společnosti pozdní doby* (Societies of a late age). Prague: SLON.

Pospíšilová, Tereza. 2013. *Jiná než ostatní. Středoevropská univerzita v Praze v letech 1990 až 1996* (Unlike any other: Central European University in Prague 1990–1996). Studies of the Hlávka Economic Institute No. 5/2013. Prague: Národohospodářský ústav Josefa Hlávky.

Potůček, Martin. 1995. Kam kráčí česká sociologie? A co jí schází? (Where is Czech sociology heading to? And what is Czech sociology missing?). *Sociologický časopis* 31 (3): 366–367.

Provazník, Stanislav et al. 1998. *Transformace vědy a výzkumu v České Republice* (The transformation of science and research in the Czech Republic). Prague: Filosofia.

Rossi, Peter. 1990. The future of sociology. *Contemporary Sociology* 19 (4): 623–624.

Seidman, Steven. 1991. The end of sociological theory: The postmodern hope. *Sociological Theory* 9 (2): 131–146.

Sokolová, Věra. 2014. Genderová studia (Gender studies). In *Dějiny české sociologie* (The history of Czech sociology), ed. Zdeněk R. Nešpor, 589–596. Prague: Academia.

Šanderová, Jadwiga. 1995. Vidím to 'trochu' jinak (I see it 'a bit' differently). *Sociologický časopis* 31 (3): 361–362.

Šiklová, Jiřina. 1990. The gray zone and the future of dissent in Czechoslovakia. *Social Research* 57 (2): 347–363.

Šmejkalová, Jiřina. 2004. Feminist sociology in the Czech Republic after 1989. *European Societies* 6 (2): 169–180.

Šubrt, Jiří. 2012. *Zpráva o činnosti Masarykovy české sociologické společnosti v letech 2009–2011* (A report on activities of the Masaryk Czech Sociological Society in 2009–2011). Available at http://www.ceskasociologicka.org/index.php/dokumenty-css/284-zprava-o-innosti-mss-v-letech-2009-2011(accessed on Dec 13, 2016).

Urbánek, Eduard. 1994. Ups and downs in Czech sociology. In *Eastern Europe in transformation: The impact on sociology*, ed. Mike Keen and Janusz Mucha, 79–88. Westport, CT: Greenwood Press.

Vohralíková, Lenka. 2002. O čem psali a bádali čeští sociologové v devadesátých letech 20. století (What have Czech sociologists researched and written in the 1990s). *Sociologický časopis/Czech Sociological Review* 38 (1–2): 139–151.

Večerník, Jiří. 1996. *Markets and people: The Czech reform experience in a comparative perspective*. Aldershot: Avebury.

Večerník, Jiří, and Petr Matějů (eds.). 1999. *Ten years of rebuilding capitalism: Czech society after 1989*. Prague: Academia.

Večerník, Jiří. 2014. Zapojení do mezinárodních empirických výzkumů (Participation in international empirical surveys). In *Dějiny české sociologie* (The history of Czech sociology), ed. Zdeněk R. Nešpor, 573–580. Prague: Academia.

Weber, Max. 1949. Objectivity in social science and social policy. In *The methodology of the social sciences*, ed. Edward Shils and Henry Finch, 50–112. Glencoe: Free Press.

CHAPTER 7

After 2000: Plugging into the European Context

Abstract After 2000, sociology in the Czech Republic expanded rapidly, especially in university settings. With the European Union accession process, new administrative regimes were introduced into the spheres of research and higher education. This chapter concentrates on the impact of external institutional factors on the development of sociology. It shows that the radical reform of national science policies after 2004 had a profound effect on sociologists' research and publication practices. The discipline's previously dominant focus on the domestic scene receded in favor of 'internationalization,' and its internal organization came to be dominated by a project-based and problem-oriented approach to research. The result is an increasingly fragmented and individualized concept of sociological inquiry.

Keywords R&D reform · Evaluation methodology · Internationalization European integration · Pluralism · Public engagement

Contrary to expectations in the 1990s, sociology in the Czech Republic has not developed autonomously since the turn of the millennium. In this chapter, we will suggest that its development has been significantly affected by the encroachment of administrative regimes that began with the science and education reforms associated primarily with the European Union accession process (the Czech Republic joined the EU in 2004). This process initiated a regime change within research and education.

M. Skovajsa and J. Balon, *Sociology in the Czech Republic*, Sociology Transformed, DOI 10.1057/978-1-137-45027-2_7

Above all, it brought external factors into play that operated irrespective of any particular disciplinary purposes. Specifically, we will trace the effects of three processes that have had a lasting impact on the development of sociology in the Czech Republic after 2000, namely expansion of the higher education sector, R&D reform, and internationalization. It will be argued that what has been crucial for sociology's latest transformations has been the external imposition of new institutional models and the lack of internal integrity, which has manifested itself as an inability to channel activities within the discipline according to its own measures.

The Boom… and Its Limits

If there was any prosperous period in the institutional history of Czech sociology, it definitely was the first decade of the 2000s. One could see signs and images of 'growth' almost everywhere: rising student enrollment, an increase in the number of study programs, an inflow of money for research, a diversity of curriculum designs, the upgrading of institutional infrastructure, and the omnipresent possibilities of international contact. In line with the overall expansion of the higher education sector, sociology departments got on track to be open to all those in search of their unlimited student choices. Irrespective of the fact that the expansion of higher education has recently ceased to be interpreted as an unequivocal 'success story,' the government policy to boost this underdeveloped and disproportionally organized sector launched it on a two-decade winning streak. In 1989, no more than about 113,000 undergraduates studied at Czech universities, but after that the number began to grow steadily until it reached 204,000 in 2001 (199,000 at public universities and 5000 at private ones).[1] By 2006, this figure had jumped to 316,000, meaning that 50% of the university-aged population was studying at higher education institutions. The sector reached its all-time high in 2010, with 396,000 students (339,000 at public universities and 57,000 at private ones). After this, the number dwindled to 327,000 in 2015, apparently due to both a declining demographic curve and new education policies favoring slogans such as 'from quantity to quality,' 'diversification,' or 'labor market relevance.'

The data for the social sciences and humanities show an even sharper increase than the overall numbers. In 1989, there were in total 4200 students enrolled in any of the social science or humanities study programs at Czech universities. This number reached 11,500 in 1996 and continued to grow rapidly, increasing from 22,500 in 2000 to 66,000 in 2012. After this, it decreased to 56,000 in 2015. Probably the strongest driving force behind this expansion was the introduction in 1992 of a 'teaching formula' as a primary mechanism for allocating public funding, which made universities dependent on an increase in student numbers (Johnstone and Marcucci 2010, p. 299). The spell of the teaching formula was weakened somewhat in the late 2000s, when this approach pushed the 'massification' process out of control, but it is still a key factor in universities' budgets.

Since 2000, the trajectory of higher education's development has been associated primarily with the implementation and specific administrative grasp of the idea of a 'research university,' which started to gain ground with the concurrent processes of plugging into the European system of science and education. Though the concept of research universities was already present in the country in the 1990s, it gained speed with the government's Act on Research and Development Support from Public Funds, which became effective in 2002 (Act No. 130/2002). As we have shown in the preceding chapters, during the communist era the relation between higher education and research had been swayed by the long-standing division of labor between the Czechoslovak Academy of Sciences and the universities in which the Academy was by law responsible for research while the universities were in charge of teaching. The 1990s removed many of the barriers resulting from this somewhat artificial division. As early as in 1990, the Higher Education Act made universities the exclusive providers of Ph.D. programs.[2] Since most of the research infrastructure had been concentrated in the Academy, which was also where postgraduate students pursued the research programs through which they earned the Soviet-era title of CSc. (*candidatus scientiarum*, which was long treated as equivalent to a Ph.D.), Ph.D. students were often formally based at a university but carried out their research at the Academy. This rather confusing situation, in which two different types of postgraduate studies coexisted side by side, was terminated by the Higher Education Act of 1998, which explicitly stated that 'only higher education institutions are allowed to award academic degrees' (Act No. 111/1998, Section 2, Par. 9). These alterations aroused a heated debate on the future directions to be taken by the Academy and the universities, with one side pointing to the 'ineffectiveness of parallel research infrastructures,' and the other praising the 'symbiosis and beneficial effects of mutual cooperation' (Šima and Pabian 2013, p. 99).

At the universities, the idea that research would be added to teaching—with both treated as separate kinds of activity—was at first met with reservations and sometimes also with open hostility (Pabian 2009; Stöckelová et al. 2009). Especially in the social science and humanities departments, the isolated rubric of 'research' appeared to be yet another way of placing demands on the university staff, which was occupied enough with the expansion of the higher education sector. Since the number of academic staff stayed more or less the same as in the 1990s and only started to grow around 2005, it was not unusual during the first decade of the new millennium for someone to teach 12 courses a week, supervise over 20 Ph.D. students or chair all manner of university boards.

The skyrocketing student enrollment can be illustrated with figures from the departments of sociology at Charles University's Faculty of Social Sciences in Prague and at Masaryk University's Faculty of Social Studies in Brno (Figs. 7.1, 7.2).[3] As these are the two largest sociology

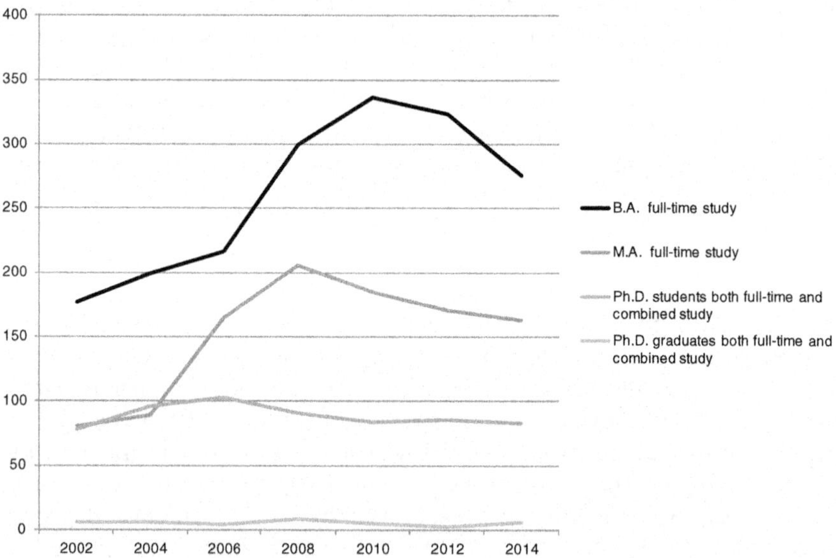

Fig. 7.1 Student enrollments and Ph.D. graduates, sociology, 2002–2014—Faculty of Social Sciences, Charles University, Prague. *Source* Annual reports of the Faculty of Social Sciences, Charles University

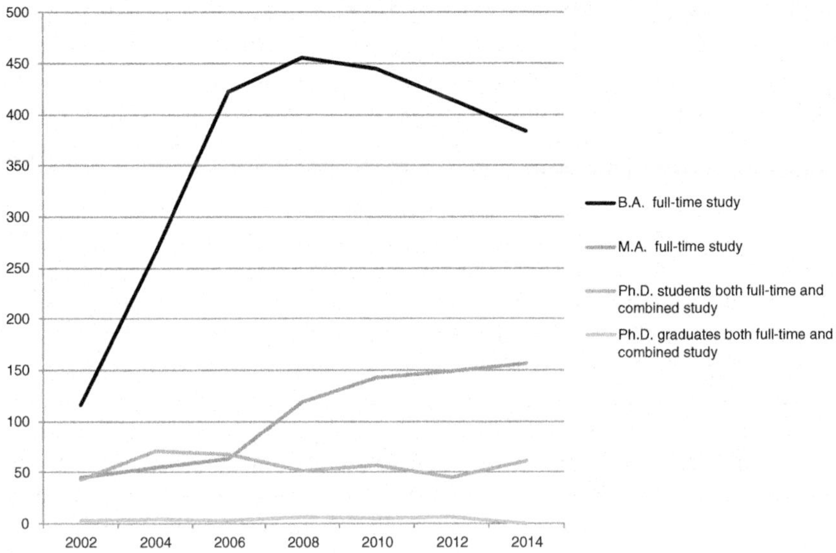

Fig. 7.2 Student enrollments and Ph.D. graduates, sociology, 2002–2014—Faculty of Social Studies, Masaryk University, Brno. *Source* Annual reports of the Faculty of Social Studies, Masaryk University. *Notes* 1. Figures for B.A. enrollments include students in joint study programs. 2. A *full-time* Ph.D. study program takes up to 4 years. The students are affiliated with a department and receive a modest government scholarship. A *combined* Ph.D. study program is designed mainly for employed students (without scholarship). After the end of the funded period, full-time students usually continue in a combined study program

departments in the country, the figures provide a good illustration of the 'boom' and its limits. However, the data are somewhat distorted by the fact that at the B.A. level they could be garnered only for sociology students in joint study programs (with social policy, journalism, political science, or other subjects). As for the general contours of the boom at the faculty level, at Brno's Faculty of Social Studies the number of sociology students rose from 621 in 1998 (when the faculty was founded) to 2359 in 2004 and 3367 in 2014. In Prague, the number climbed from 2413 in 2000 to 3033 in 2006 and 4461 in 2015. The Prague faculty's budget increased from an equivalent of €2.7 million in 2002 (15% of this sum was for research) to €7.1 million in 2006 (30% for research) and €12.6 million in 2015 (25%). The figures for Brno show a similarly expanding budget: from €2.6 million in 2002 (33% for research) to €6.4 million in 2006 (22%) and €10.6 million in 2014 (24%).[4]

As suggested by the figures for sociology departments and for the faculties as a whole, the student 'boom' climaxed around 2008–2010. Since then there has been a significant downward trend, especially in B.A. study programs, which were reduced by new government policies implemented in 2009. As far as sociology is concerned, these regulatory changes coincided with declining student interest in sociology as a major. The number of applications to the B.A. sociology program at the Faculty of Social Sciences in Prague fell from a peak of 1567 in 2008 to 739 in 2012 and 325 in 2015; in Brno, the numbers dropped from 1877 in 2007 to 839 in 2014. This decline in student interest meant that the faculties had to 'hunt' for students and had to reinterpret education in terms of its exchange value and applicability on the labor market.

Once the higher education 'boom' reached its limit, the time came for sociologists to reflect on what this 'happy wave' had brought them and whether it perhaps was the case that, to quote Lord Byron, it had 'repassed them in its flow.' This concern gets even more serious if we consider how few there were of the 'few' who ought to be serving the 'many.' A simple look at the academic staff reveals that at the department of sociology in Brno in 2008, there were three professors, two associate professors (docents) and seven Ph.D.s serving a contingent of 626 students (the number has risen since the end of the boom: from 2, 9 and 13 in 2012 to 3, 7 and 17 in 2014). Although during the conjuncture sociology departments at Czech universities definitely expanded their teaching capacities, developed their long-term research focus, established new research centers, and became active in many projects, it is still true that all this took place in the absence of any shared vision of the discipline's standing vis-à-vis the processes under way in the areas of research and education. The departments rode the 'happy wave' passively, following the movements of the tide.

The constant pressure from policy makers and university management to open up new possibilities for students resulted in a plethora of study combinations that were often accredited unhesitatingly, just for the sake of not missing the 'opportunity.' For a long time, sociology, as a traditional subject, profited from the interest on the part of the 'new' social studies to form joint study programs. At first, these disciplines needed sociology for accreditation purposes. But after they had attained a stronger institutional position, especially thanks to intensive student demand and greater labor market relevance, their interest faded away. Initially, the study programs were, almost without exception, offered in the form of 'sociology and….' This habit is now more and more in retreat, and programs such as 'media studies and sociology' are coming onto the scene. As John Holmwood (2010) has suggested in the British context, the rise of the new, mainly applied, social studies has probably been inevitable. These programs seem to have the upper hand in the open competition for students.

We can conclude this section by saying that university-based sociology in the Czech Republic is currently hanging in the balance. After two decades of massive institutional 'growth,' the discipline is facing a period of 'no growth.' It remains to be seen what effect these adverse conditions will have on its further direction. For the time being, it is still a discipline after the 'boom,' not a discipline in 'crisis.'

Under the Surveillance of Administrative Databases

As we have argued in Chap. 6, in the 1990s the state and its regulatory bodies exerted very modest direct political or ideological influence on the formation of sociology's disciplinary agenda. Since 2000, new systems of governance have come into existence, with profound effects on the discipline's internal organization. To avoid being reminiscent of the ideological control and political manipulation of the communist era, these new instruments of external regulation were presented as a 'depoliticized' and 'depersonalized' (Arnold 2011) form of research policy. The regulatory framework introduced after 2000, which focused on the effective management of public funds, was essentially a Czech interpretation of Western science policies that relied on a very simple and apparently post-ideological vocabulary, taken primarily from Western reform plans (and from various international comparative studies of research productivity using EU and OECD indicators). Western institutional models for the organization of research and higher education, as well as guiding concepts, such as 'excellence,' 'applicability,' 'efficiency,' 'links to industry,' have had a specific following in the Czech Republic, eventually forming 'what is arguably the most radical performance-based evaluation system in Europe' (Young 2014, p. 15).

The first National Research and Development Policy, launched in 2000, proved to be a genuine operational tool for transforming the Czech academic environment. Its main objectives involved the formation of an 'evaluation' culture and the introduction of objective performance indicators into the area of research in the Czech Republic. Academic autonomy and self-governance were to be limited in line with the then-prevalent argument that they were the cause of 'nepotism, corruption and lobbying' (Good et al. 2015, p. 94). As a follow-up to the emerging R&D frame of reference, new 'performance-based' regulatory tools came into existence, most notably the Evaluation Methodology in 2004. This methodology turned out to be a determining factor of the direction taken by research in the Czech Republic for many years to come, as it was linked to a particular practice of scientometric calculation of a research product's 'value.' Research institutions, including universities, uploaded all of their eligible research outputs into a centralized R&D information system (the Information Register of R&D Outputs, RIV). Each research output (mainly publications, patents, prototypes, government-certified procedures) generated a certain number of 'points'—determined by the specific research output category—for the institution which had registered it. The results were then (and in many cases still are) used as a basis for allocating funding on a yearly basis. The methodology overtly favored 'hard sciences' and 'attributed disproportionately higher point scores to high-impact journals and certain types of patents (the journals Nature, Science, and PNAS, and patents in the US, Japan, and Europe…)' (Linková 2014, p. 82).

On a number of counts, the Evaluation Methodology epitomized the whole reform process. It was designed as a simple cure for complex diseases. Since it is updated every year, it has introduced another source of instability and unpredictability into the system. Starting from a simple scheme of just three output categories, it eventually turned into a complicated and impenetrable collection of almost any 'research output' a person could imagine (26 categories in 2010). In general terms, the idea behind the Evaluation Methodology was 'an attempt to depersonalize resource allocation through the use of arithmetic because many feel that individual people cannot be trusted to make impartial and objective decisions' (Arnold 2011, p. 53).

Although announced as an objective and impartial device, the political legitimization of the new research evaluation model rested largely on economic grounds, since it converged with the notion of the coming 'knowledge' economy in which 'knowledge' was broadly understood as a commodity and its 'production' as an investment.[5] In a matter of only a few years, the Czech research environment changed (almost) beyond recognition. In stark contrast to the situation in the early 2000s, when most academics in the Czech Republic apparently did not follow changes in science policy, nobody was surprised that the 2008 R&D reform 'transformed research accountability from an enclosed professional system governed by academic peer-review into an administrative assessment carried out by the government' (Linková and Stöckelová 2012, p. 625). What made the R&D reform truly effective was the fact that the 'scoring' system immediately brought a new understanding of scientific productivity and, even more significantly, changed the way in which academics viewed themselves. Within the social sciences and humanities, knowledge production was identified almost exclusively with the production of publications within the eligible categories.

The Evaluation Methodology also had a direct influence on the (self-) definition of particular academic disciplines. When entering a publication into the R&D information system, the author and her institution had to categorize it as the product of a particular discipline (from a list of eligible ones). This way of determining disciplinary 'relevance' resulted in a new 'coherent' community of sociologists. To put it simply, what is registered under 'sociology' is a product of sociology in the Czech Republic. Such a purely technical definition of disciplinary affiliation might seem sorely insufficient at a time when many voices from the leading traditions are pointing to a continuing 'identity crisis' among sociologists (Crane and Small 1992; Holmwood 2014; Turner 2014) or a need to 'reconceptualize knowledge accumulation in sociology' (Abbott 2006). On top of that, the new scoring system has also intensified the sense of malaise among Czech sociologists by demonstrating that their 'productivity' and 'efficiency' is unsatisfactory in comparison with other disciplines. Sociology (unlike philosophy, law, political science, or anthropology) has fallen under an evaluation regime very similar to the one applied to the natural and technical sciences.

What, then, was the outcome of Czech sociology's confrontation with the new regulatory system? One obvious consequence was that

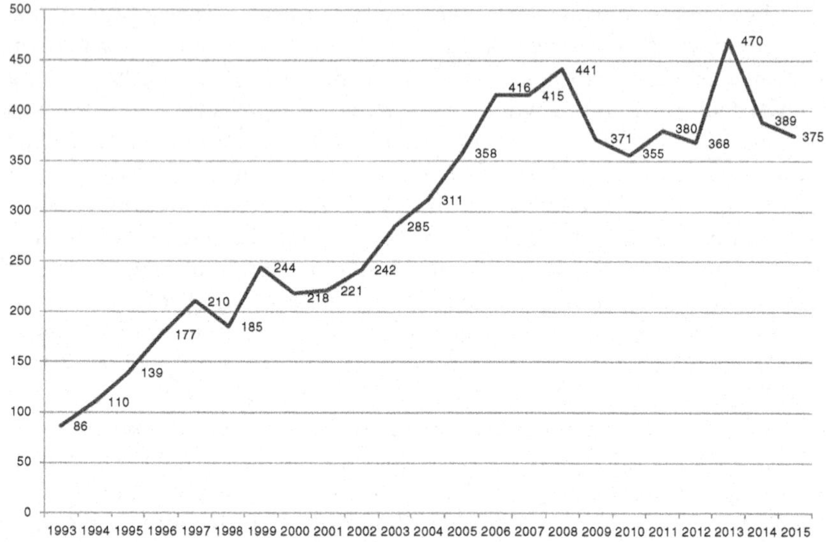

Fig. 7.3 Number of research outputs (books, book chapters, journal articles), sociology and demography, 1993–2015. *Source* Czech Republic's information register of R&D outputs (RIV)

research—or, more precisely, the production of publications—invaded higher education settings, and educational matters were overshadowed by a sudden concern with creating a research environment at the universities. Although the imperative of 'research-led' teaching has produced only sporadic results in sociology so far, the evaluation system imposed the notion of 'research' as a strictly project-based and problem-oriented undertaking. In line with the general outburst of publication productivity (as measured by the available metrics), which at the country's universities grew by 65% in 2009, by 30% in 2010 and by 12% in 2011 (Fiala 2013), sociologists in the Czech Republic revved up their publication activity. As evidenced by Fig. 7.3, they did not stand in the way of change responding promptly to the new demands.[6]

To a large extent, the trajectory of publication productivity of Czech sociology coincides with the effects of policy changes in the R&D area. The first significant increase around 1999 corresponds to the introduction of the so-called Research Intentions in 1998, which were conceived as 'forward-looking plans, explaining how research organizations intended to use institutional research funding to reach specific institutional objectives' (Good et al. 2015, p. 93). Essentially, these plans represented the first state-organized attempt at 'strategic planning' and for a long time were believed to be the vanguard of the practice of institutional funding. Another sharp increase, starting around 2005, coincides with the implementation of the 2004 Evaluation Methodology. One possible, optimistic, interpretation of the recent declining trend that set in after 2013 is that it represents a nod to the turn from 'quantity to quality' and is consistent with the growing tendency to publish in higher-ranked journals and with renowned publishers.

By upsetting the status quo, the R&D reform had a big upside in its continued push to get the stagnating area of research moving again. On the other hand, it represented a harsh, externally imposed intervention into the system, which had enjoyed just a decade of relative autonomy. The reform gave rise to many pathologies, most notably system gaming, the mass production of low-quality publications, and the use of productivity measures as a means of coercive power directed at academic staff. With the introduction of austerity measures in 2008, 'open competition' often tended to revert to 'the survival of the fittest.'

The administrative databases introduced as part of the new research evaluation system created an unexpected external audience for sociology's products and had a major impact on the internal organization of the discipline, which became thoroughly adapted to the policy regime associated with them. However, the mere existence of the databases had a detrimental effect inasmuch as they diverted sociologists' attention away from the major questions of the scientific, educational, and public relevance of their discipline. The idea that sociology would stand or fall depending on the volume of 'output' it produced is, of course, one-sided and not viable in the long run as it is disconnected from any consideration of the disciplinary purpose. In many respects, living in the shadow of silent databases abruptly terminated the deceptive and often naïve projections of sociologists in the 1990s, who had hoped that their discipline would enjoy continuity, autonomy and slow but sustained growth.

Internationalized, Finally?

Although the imperative of 'internationalization' had a rather profane meaning under the communist regime (given its association with various slogans of the workers' movement), it entered the post-1989 vocabulary quite naturally. Symbolically, it was associated with the image of removing the barbed wire from the geographical border with the West, which had previously been guarded by armed soldiers and could only be crossed at the risk of life. In the academic sphere, 'internationalization' assumed a preeminent place right after 'the changing of the guard'. Ever since then, it has become one of the most tenacious mantras in both research and education policy. After an initial, mostly intuitive, spontaneous and enthusiastic absorption with 'learning from the West' and imitating Western academic culture—as the situation in the 1990s could be characterized—'internationalization' invaded academic settings in the form of bureaucratic regulations and sets of indicators systematically aimed at integrating Czech academia into the European research and education environment. Because the major European policy documents in this area such as the Bologna Declaration and the Lisbon Strategy provided no specific guidelines for the countries that had been absent from the complex integration processes going on in the West for many decades, the will to conform to the new demands was often in stark contrast to the ability to meet expectations.

It wasn't until the 2000s that 'internationalization,' now the battle cry of governments determined to consolidate the areas of research and education in compliance with the fashionable vision of a 'Europe of Knowledge,' acquired its present top-down character and began to encroach on Czech academic institutions' autonomy. The vicissitudes of the state's appropriation of this agenda reached their peak in the 2008 reform plan elaborated by the government's Council for Research and Development—at the time headed by the center-right Prime Minister Mirek Topolánek—which bore the motto 'we will only do what we are number one or number two at in the world' (Council for Research and Development 2007, p. 6), unwittingly reiterating Jack Welch's plans to reorganize General Electric. Although the scarecrow later put on more fancy clothes, this economistic viewpoint and the refrain of national competiveness continue to occupy a central position:

> Apart from traditional characteristics such as independence, rationality and objectivity, other values are coming into the forefront nowadays due to the changes in science policy, such as usability, excellence, interdisciplinarity, international cooperation and mobility. These new values contribute to the improvement of our country's competitiveness, which is also one of the main priorities of the government. (Council for Research and Development 2011, p. 4)

The endless sequence of reform plans,[7] typically announced (every year) as the 'final' ones, only to be repeatedly amended, recalled, and replaced by ever newer ones, did little to reduce the instability of the Czech academic environment, whose institutions learned to operate in a double-edged reality: on the one hand, they were required to formulate long-term plans and objectives, but on the other they lived in constant uncertainty regarding the upcoming year (and the always tentative budget). Naturally, one effect of the mantra of national competitiveness was the heightening of domestic competitive tensions—specifically, between the universities and the Academy of Sciences, between the traditional universities and the more recently established regional ones, and between particular faculties or departments.

Whether in the form of administrative rubrics or measurable indicators, 'internationalization' has had a deep effect on student and academic mobility, promotion criteria, research production, publication strategies, job appointments, and, generally, on the formation of an academic culture. In a matter of only a few years, things changed quite dramatically. There is a sharp divide between what had been possible, let's say, in 2005, and what was possible in 2010 or 2015. As late as the mid-2000s, one could reach 'even the highest ranks of the academic hierarchy without publishing abroad: at the time of promotion, 85% of professors and 89% of associate professors of economics did not have a single article in a journal published abroad to their name' (Melichar and Pabian 2007, p. 48; Macháček and Kolcunová 2005). Other negative features of Czech academic life, such as inbreeding, multiple professorial appointments for accreditation purposes, or pre-selection of job candidates (Tollingerová and Šebková 1995; Tucker 2000; Stöckelová et al. 2009), have also been on the decline since the late 2000s, thanks to new administrative rules that favored open competition and Western academic customs.

As shown in Chap. 6, the 1990s were a period of intellectual 'reception.' At last, sociologists in the Czech Republic were free to learn about Western ideas, theories, and methods. In the 2000s, with the arrival of the new administrative regime, its central registers and other regulatory devices, they were confronted with Western-type institutional arrangements and the new attendant pressures. How, then, did sociologists in the Czech Republic (a group still basically identical with 'Czech sociologists') perform under the new institutional conditions? According to the data from the Web of Science (WoS), in 1998–2007 Czech sociologists—at the time affiliated with one of the country's 17 departments and research institutes engaged in sociological research—published 200 articles (by 108 authors) in WoS-indexed journals from the category of 'narrowly focused sociology journals, out of which a total of 170 were published in the *Sociologický časopis/Czech Sociological Review*' (Basl et al. 2009, p. 8). Czech sociologists' virtual absence from international scholarly exchange was characteristic of publication practice before the arrival of the government's research reform plan. A more recent study that also included the data from the national Information Register of R&D outputs provides an overview for the 2008–2012 period (Jurajda and Münich 2015). The study points to a significant increase in the number of articles published in WoS-indexed sociological journals (174), as well as a continuing trend to publish in lower-ranked journals—only 15 articles were in the category of international journals with a high impact factor. The bilingual journal *Sociologický časopis/Czech Sociological Review* continues to represent the most frequent single publication platform for Czech sociologists. Despite the existence of an English edition, the review's audience remains mostly domestic. Less than one third (29%) of the articles citing this journal in the WoS in 2006–2013 were from non-Czech (or non-Slovak) journals, but almost half of those articles were written by Czech or Slovak authors (Skovajsa 2014, p. 692).

The internationalization of sociology in the Czech Republic, or at least its increased visibility on the international scene, can also be traced using other indicators such as student and academic staff mobility, membership in international associations, or the number of study programs and courses taught in English. Just one (rising) number among many: in the 1990s, only one Czech student of sociology was awarded a Fulbright scholarship for research or study in the United States, whereas in the period from 2000 to 2016, the Fulbright Commission in Prague granted 24 (out of 590) student or research scholarships to sociologists.[8] A similar trend applies to the Marie Curie Fellowships and other forms of international mobility.

Also growing is the presence of Czech sociologists in the International Sociological Association (ISA), and, even more so, in the European Sociological Association (ESA)—of which the former director of the Prague campus of the Central European University Jiří Musil served as president in 1998–2001. In 2015, the Czech Academy of Sciences' Institute of Sociology hosted ESA's 12th conference in Prague, with dozens of participants from the Czech Republic. Two Czech sociologists, Tomáš Kostelecký and Csaba Szaló, are currently members of ESA's executive committee.

Czech sociologists' slow but steady penetration of the discipline's international structures contrasts with the widespread absence of non-Czech sociologists (disregarding a handful of positive exceptions) from the country's sociological institutions. Probably the most powerful obstacle to Czech sociological departments achieving a more international profile is the current level of salaries. Czech wages are generally low in an EU-wide comparison (average net wage under €800 as compared to the EU-28 average of €1500 in 2015), and this disparity is reflected in academic salaries as well. Salaries for young entrants into the academic field tend to be around €600/month (full-time, net), but they are low also for professors, beginning from as little as €950/month (net). Researcher salaries are currently set at €900/month (net) by the Czech Science Foundation (GA ČR). With salaries this low, Czech academic jobs might have some attraction for Western postdocs facing the risk of unemployment at home, but established academics usually treat offers from Czech institutions as a bad joke. The influx of EU structural funds after 2004 boosted salaries everywhere except in Prague (which, as an affluent region, does not qualify for most EU funds), but this source of funding is only temporary, involves extreme bureaucracy, and has often been used in chaotic ways. Another factor keeping foreign academics from moving to Czech institutions is the fact that the Czech Republic does not recognize the highest academic degrees (docent, professor) from abroad.

To summarize, one obvious consequence of Czech academia's confrontation with the critical mantras of the new research policy (such as 'world-class science,' 'research-led teaching,' 'international expertise,' or 'publicly relevant knowledge') has been the appropriation of Western institutional models. It was not the 'intellectual' import of Western ideas that has been foundational in the last 25 years. Rather, it was the importation of institutional models and practices that proved to be crucial for sociology in the Czech Republic during its most recent period of development. With the adoption of these models, Czech sociology finally became 'internationalized,' began to be measured by the standards of the European research and education environment, and detached itself from the initial aspirations and concerns of its 1990s 'reawakening.' Such an externally imposed transformation, of course, will have a downside as well. While original research could be all too easily defined as the production of publications within the appropriate administrative rubrics, the discipline's quest for intellectual purpose and public relevance remained unfulfilled. No less seriously, Czech sociology's adaptation to the new international knowledge regimes appears to be both reinforcing and fostering the discipline's traditional weaknesses, namely anti-intellectualism, aversion to theory, descriptive orientation,[9] eclecticism, and an emphasis on narrow practical application (Musil 2002; Petrusek 2011).

This notwithstanding, the new regulatory practice has had many positive effects on sociology's consolidation in the Czech Republic, for instance, in terms of standardizing promotion criteria, styles of writing, funding arrangements, or maintaining disciplinary boundaries. One optimistic interpretation of the bizarre notion that publications translate into funding income might be that it created a situation in which publishing finally got the respect it deserved in sociology and other social sciences. By so vehemently favoring international output, meaning articles and other publications intended for the English-speaking Western academic sphere, this system has brought a new audience—with its well-established publication culture—into play. And maybe most importantly for the social sciences in the Czech Republic, it has introduced binding performance criteria into disciplines that for the previous several decades had been used to operating on a promissory basis.

Pluralist and Fragmented

If there is one notion most reflective of Czech sociology's recent history, it is probably 'pluralism'. Czech sociologists embraced this concept right after 1989, partly due to their persisting memory of the notion of 'dominant,' 'official,' or 'unified' sociology, and partly due to their uncertainty concerning the basic means and goals of sociology. The understanding of sociological inquiry as the unrestricted study of things one is interested in has been widely employed especially in university settings, where it makes up a substantial part of the discipline's appeal for students. In the 1990s, the progressive inclusion of new concepts, methods, approaches, sub-disciplines, study programs, courses, and so on was viewed as a positive sign of the discipline's colorfulness. With the arrival of the research and higher education reforms after 2000, Czech sociology's pluralism further increased. Through their universally applicable criteria, the reforms had a profound effect on disciplinary agendas. With their stress on individual 'research' productivity and variety in educational options, they promoted both the fragmentation of research interests and the proliferation of study courses. No sociology department in the Czech Republic can be said to have an integrated disciplinary profile. On the whole, the situation bears many similarities to the 1990s. However, this recent 'fragmentation' results not only from the discipline's intellectual and social organization, but increasingly also from the shift toward more managerial and bureaucratic forms of academic governance.

Both the large traditional universities and the young universities based in the regional centers have worked hard to develop their unique research profiles. Next to their long-standing preoccupations (listed in Chap. 6), the traditional departments have more recently taken interest in widely varying new research specializations: 'political movements,' 'medical sociology,' and 'collective memory' (Prague's Faculty of Social Sciences); the practically oriented fields of 'socio-economic evaluation' and 'data analysis' (Prague's Faculty of Arts); 'cultural sociology,' 'social inequality,' and 'migration' (Brno's Faculty of Social Studies); 'aging,' 'lifestyles,' 'social exclusion,' and 'education' (the Faculty of Arts in Olomouc). Typically, the continuity of research or educational activities is evidence more of long-term individual interests of particular sociologists than of institutionally orchestrated collaborative efforts. The more recently founded university departments have had a much shorter time to craft a specific research profile, but they nevertheless have developed their own areas of specialization: 'sociology of religion' or 'gender, family and health' (Plzeň), 'regional development' (Hradec Králové), and 'civil society' (Ostrava).

The number of courses on offer at sociology departments in the Czech Republic is typically very high, covering a multitude of disciplinary approaches and various interdisciplinary combinations. On the whole, the discipline has adopted an identity emphasizing its all-encompassing nature. The role of sociology is to satisfy the needs of all parties involved and to provide a multidisciplinary education as well as specialized knowledge skills. This 'master of all trades' concept of the discipline is also reflected in the thematic foci of the top national research organization, the Institute of Sociology at the Academy of Sciences. The Institute, which currently employs around 100 researchers on a full-time or part-time basis, pursues research activities in nearly 50 areas.[10] Although most of its researchers work in rather traditional areas such as 'economic sociology,' 'political sociology,' or 'public opinion,' the supremacy of project-based funding transcends any disciplinary divisions. Thus, for example, a historian of Czech sociology and religious life is affiliated with the department of economic sociology, or a junior researcher specializing in philosophical hermeneutics works at the Institute's Public Opinion Research Centre on projects as diverse as 'the application of philosophical hermeneutics to the sociological theory of intersubjectivity' and 'the social aspects of nuclear energy.'

In contrast to the situation in the 1990s and 2000s, when key positions in the discipline were occupied by sociologists in their 50s to 70s, in recent years most of the discipline's leadership have been members of the 40-something generation born in the 1960s or 1970s. The central figures of the post-1989 renewal (most notably Pavel Machonin, Ivo Možný, Jiří Musil, Miloslav Petrusek) have passed away, and many other protagonists of the 'transformation' period have either retired or left the profession. However, it would be incorrect to suggest that, after so many decades of generational instability, sociology in the Czech Republic has experienced a standard changing of the guard. The middle-aged generation's absence from important positions in the 1990s, which resulted from the distorted mechanism of academic reproduction under Normalization and from the economic pressures of the transformation period, naturally translated into their absence from senior academic staff in the last decade. In the late 2000s, over the course of just a few years, the leading disciplinary positions were taken over by the cohort born in 1965–1975, often for the simple reason that the many newly vacated institutional positions had to be filled by someone. With the rapid expansion of higher education and the implementation of R&D reform, these new institutional leaders were exposed to growing administrative burdens. Completing habilitation, or sometimes even just a Ph.D., was often rewarded with heavy involvement in department or faculty management, commission memberships, chairmanship of committees, evaluation procedures, accreditation processes, or supervision and administration of study programs.

As evidenced by the data from the national database of professors and docents (associate professors),[11] there are now 10 professors and 27 docents of sociology active in the Czech higher education system. Out of these, eight professors and 20 docents were appointed after 2000. Given the expansion of the system, their engagement has primarily taken the form of activities that have more to do with institutional development and the discipline's maintenance than with the tasks of intellectual leadership. Likewise, and with the notable exception of Jan Keller, professor of sociology at the universities in Brno and Ostrava (and a member of the European Parliament for the Czech Social Democratic Party since 2014), the political or public engagement of sociologists in the Czech Republic after 2000 has revolved around particular visions of the development of research and education rather than broader political issues. Petr Matějů, one of the key protagonists of the 1990s 'transformation' debate (see Chap. 6), was an architect of the higher education reform pushed, without success, by the center-right government in the late 2000s. In 2008, he became the president of the main national funding body for basic research, the Czech Science Foundation, and launched its major reorganization in line with the R&D reform. Several Czech sociologists of opposite ideological leanings took the other stance and participated in the anti-reform movement called 'Science is alive.' Its campaign culminated in August 2009, when some 1000 people gathered for a demonstration in support of 'science'—arguably the largest ever in the Czech lands (see Linková 2014, p. 83). It was also one of the rare occasions when sociologists in the Czech Republic entered the public debate with the intention to challenge the processes under way and not only to comment on them.

In general, however, there seem to be few, if any, open ideological conflicts within today's sociology in the Czech Republic. The generational shift passed off placidly, which, again, might be explained by reference to the 'missing generation.' As there is no disciplinary consensus, there is no point in challenging the status quo. Under the current knowledge regime, the institutional 'position' of sociology obviously precedes its disciplinary or intellectual 'identity.' Seen from an institutional perspective, the discipline has grown considerably in size in the last 15 years. It is becoming internationally visible and is increasingly organized in accordance with international (Western) standards, but the 'gap' with the West still persists. In what can seem an ultimate irony, it is, thus, rather on the intellectual level, where it would seem that the state of sociology in the Czech Republic has begun to resemble very closely the ups and downs of sociology in the Western countries. Both as a research discipline and an educational program, it is decentralized, highly pluralized, individualized, fragmented, and defending itself against various forms of marginalization. In this respect, it is indisputably reconnected with the West.

Conclusion

In many ways, the recent history of sociology in the Czech Republic exemplifies the plight of small national traditions. Michael Burawoy may be justified in calling for 'provincializing the social sciences' (Burawoy 2005) or rejecting the 'hegemonic strategy of the dominant' (Burawoy 2016, p. 951), but such calls are related to 'intellectual' imperialism rather than to the importation and administrative encroachment of Western institutional models. The current state of Czech sociology indicates that the dependence on external authorities and on the concomitant vagaries of changing administrative regimes results in (or aggravates) the lack of internal disciplinary integrity. The intellectual concerns regarding the discipline's purpose are sidelined inasmuch as it is primarily the institutional interventions that have structured the environment in which sociology is located.

As we have suggested in this chapter, sociology in the Czech Republic now exists in an environment that tends to understand scientific disciplines as producers of knowledge. Despite recent attempts to study epistemic activities within the social sciences not only in terms of the processes of 'knowledge production, application and evaluation,' but also more in line with their own historically formed approaches (Camic et al. 2011), the natural science model still reigns supreme and has had an all-pervading influence on the way in which 'knowledge production' is construed today. The challenge—then presumably not only for Czech sociology but for other national traditions as well—is to be sensitive to all those processes that are undermining the central legacies of the discipline, now considered outdated and unsuitable: criticism, reflexivity, creativity, solidarity, and cohesion. Not so long after the battle for enforcing 'unified' science had died down, the image of the one and only relevant science turned up anew, this time as a 'world-class' science. If knowledge cannot be universal, it can at least be 'groundbreaking.'

Of course, it would be too early to estimate what effect this understanding of research in terms of knowledge 'production, application, and evaluation' will have on the still rather hazy state of sociology in the Czech Republic. In any case, it is likely that its fortune will depend on what is deemed relevant by external audiences rather than by sociologists themselves.

Notes

1. All following student numbers are adapted from statistical records of the Czech Ministry of Education, Youth and Sports: http://www.msmt.cz/vzdelavani/skolstvi-v-cr/statistika-skolstvi/terciarni-vzdelavani (accessed on Dec 13, 2016).
2. This Act also introduced now standard types of study programs (B.A., M.A., and Ph.D. level).
3. The picture of student growth would not be complete without mentioning that in addition to the departments in Prague, Brno and Olomouc, in the 2000s new sociology programs and departments were established at the universities in the regional cities of Plzeň, Hradec Králové and Ostrava.
4. All data are adapted from the annual reports of the Faculty of Social Sciences (Prague) and Faculty of Social Studies (Brno).
5. The R&D reform was approved by the government in 2008 with the motto: 'Science makes knowledge from money, innovation makes money from knowledge' (Council for Research and Development 2008).
6. In terms of the key eligible outputs (journal articles, monographs, and chapters in a monograph), in 2008–2015 sociologists in the Czech Republic (along with the much smaller community of demographers who share the same category with sociologists) registered a total of 2129 articles (as compared to 1767 in 1998–2007), 446 monographs (525 in 1998–2007) and 2269 chapters (1932 in 1998–2007) in the central research output register, RIV. See https://www.rvvi.cz/riv.
7. Some of the reform plans provoked strong public reaction if they included proposals that were seen as alien to Czech traditions, such as the attempt to introduce student fees at public universities in 2010.
8. The data were provided by the Prague office of the Fulbright Commission.
9. Some observers have noted a characteristic 'factographic' inclination towards the accumulation and presentation of facts as 'bits of objective information without engaging in explicit interpretations of those facts' (Bryant 2000, p. 40).
10. See http://www.soc.cas.cz/en (accessed on Oct 20, 2016).
11. REDOP, see https://www.redop.cz (accessed on Dec 13, 2016).

References

Abbott, Andrew. 2006. Reconceptualizing knowledge accumulation in sociology. *The American Sociologist* 37 (2): 57–66.

Act 111/1998. 1998. *Higher education act.* Prague: Parliament of the Czech Republic.

Arnold, Erik. 2011. *International audit of research, development & innovation in the Czech Republic: Synthesis report*. Brighton: Technopolis Group.

Basl, Josef, Daniel Münich, and Oleg Sidorkin. 2009. Publication productivity of Czech sociology in scientific journals within the last decade. CERGE-EI Working Paper Series No. 392, CERGE-EI, Prague.

Bryant, Chad. 2000. Whose nation? Czech dissidents and history writing from a post-1989 perspective. *History and Memory* 12 (1): 30–64.

Burawoy, Michael. 2005. Provincializing the social sciences. In *The politics of method in the human sciences: Positivism and its epistemological others*, ed. George Steinmetz, 508–525. Durham, NC: Duke University Press.

Burawoy, Michael. 2016. The promise of sociology: Global challenges for national disciplines. *Sociology* 50 (5): 949–959.

Camic, Charles, Neil Gross, and Michèle Lamont (eds.). 2011. *Social knowledge in the making*. Chicago: University of Chicago Press.

Council for Research and Development. 2007. *Analysis of the existing state of research, development and innovation in the Czech Republic and a comparison with the situation abroad in 2007*. Prague: Office of the Government.

Council for Research and Development. 2008. *Reform of the research, development and innovation system in the Czech Republic (approved by the Government Resolution No. 287 of 26 March 2008)*. Prague: Office of the Government.

Council for Research and Development. 2011. *Analysis of the existing state of research, development and innovation in the Czech Republic and a comparison with the situation abroad in 2011*. Prague: Office of the Government.

Crane, Diana, and Henry Small. 1992. American sociology since the seventies: The emerging identity crisis in the discipline. In *Sociology and its publics: the forms and fates of disciplinary organization*, ed. Terence C. Halliday and Morris Janowitz, 197–235. Chicago: University of Chicago Press.

Fiala, Dalibor. 2013. Science evaluation in the Czech Republic: The case of universities. *Societies* 3 (3): 266–279.

Good, Barbara, Niki Vermeleuen, Briggite Tiefenthaler, and Erik Arnold. 2015. Counting quality? The Czech performance-based research funding system. *Research Evaluation* 24 (2): 91–105.

Holmwood, John. 2010. Sociology's misfortune: Disciplines, interdisciplinarity and the impact of audit culture. *British Journal of Sociology* 61 (4): 639–658.

Holmwood, John. 2014. Sociology's past and futures: The impact of external structure, policy and financing. In *The Palgrave handbook of sociology in Britain*, ed. John Holmwood and John Scott, 588–610. Basingstoke: Palgrave Macmillan.

Johnstone, D. Bruce, and Pamela Marcucci. 2010. *Financing higher education worldwide: Who pays? Who should pay?* Baltimore: The Johns Hopkins University Press.

Jurajda, Štěpán, and Daniel Münich. 2015. *Oborová publikační výkonnost pracovišť výzkumných organizací v České republice v letech 2008–2012* (Czech research centres' publication performance in the period 2008–2012, by field of research). Prague: Economics Institute of the Czech Academy of Sciences.

Linková, Marcela. 2014. Unable to resist: Researchers' responses to research assessment in the Czech Republic. *Human Affairs* 24 (1): 78–88.

Linková, Marcela, and Tereza Stöckelová. 2012. Public accountability and the politicization of science: The peculiar journey of Czech research assessment. *Science and Public Policy* 39 (5): 618–629.

Macháček, Martin, and Eva Kolcunová. 2005. Jak se v ČR žije kandidátům na docenty a profesory? Analýza publikačních aktivit v ekonomických disciplínách [Publish or perish: On the importance of publishing for the economic sciences tenure-track in the CR]. *Finance a úvěr/Czech Journal of Economics and Finance* 55 (11–12): 563–577.

Melichar, Marek, and Petr Pabian. 2007. Czech Republic—Shifting peripheries: A state of the art report on the Czech academic profession. In *The changing conditions for academic work and careers in select countries*, ed. William Locke and Ulrich Teichler, 39–56. Kassel: International Centre for Higher Education Research.

Musil, Jiří. 2002. Zamyšlení nad soudobou českou sociologií (Some comments on contemporary Czech sociology). *Sociologický časopis/Czech Sociological Review* 38 (1–2): 17–24.

Pabian, Petr. 2009. Europeanization of higher education governance in the post-communist context: the case of Czech Republic. In *European integration and the governance of higher education and research*, ed. Alberto Amaral et al., 257–278. Dodrecht: Springer.

Petrusek, Miloslav. 2011. Návrat (sociologické) teorie do Čech? Východiska, stav a perspektivy (The return of (sociological) theory to the Czech Republic? Principles, perspectives, and current status). *Sociologický časopis/Czech Sociological Review* 47 (5): 1017–1034.

Šima, Karel, and Petr Pabian. 2013. *Ztracený Humboldtův ráj: Ideologie jednoty výzkumu a výuky ve vysokém školství* (Humboldt's paradise lost: The ideology of Einheit von Forschung und Lehre in higher education). Prague: SLON.

Skovajsa, Marek. 2014. Celková a zahraniční citovanost Sociologického časopisu: výsledky citační analýzy (Total and foreign-journal citedness of Sociologický časopis: The results of a citation analysis). *Sociologický časopis/Czech Sociological Review* 50 (5): 671–712.

Stöckelová, Tereza, et al. 2009. *Akademické poznávání, vykazování a podnikání. Etnografie měnící se české vědy* (Czech science in flux: Etnography of making, administering and enterprising knowledge in the academy). Prague: SLON.

Tollingerová, Dana, and Helena Šebková. 1995. The Czech higher education institutions and their staffing policy. *Higher Education Management* 7 (2): 229–240.

Tucker, Aviezer. 2000. Reproducing incompetence: The constitution of Czech higher education. *East European Constitutional Review* 9 (3): 94–99.

Turner, Stephen. 2014. *American sociology: From pre-disciplinary to post-normal.* Basingstoke: Palgrave Macmillan.

Young, Mitchell. 2014. Coarsely ground: Developing the Czech system of research evaluation. In *Global challenges, local responses in higher education: The contemporary issues in national and comparative perspective*, ed. Jelena Branković, Manja Klementić, Predrag Lažetić, and Pavel Zgaga, 15–34. Rotterdam: Sense Publishers.

Index

M. Skovajsa and J. Balon, *Sociology in the Czech Republic*, Sociology Transformed, DOI 10.1057/978-1-137-45027-2

Printed by Printforce, the Netherlands